Day-by-Day Math Thinking Routines in Second Grade

Day-by-Day Math Thinking Routines in Second Grade helps you provide students with a review of the foundational ideas in math, every day of the week! Based on the bestselling *Daily Math Thinking Routines in Action*, the book follows the simple premise that frequent, rigorous, engaging practice leads to mastery and retention of concepts, ideas, and skills. These worksheet-free, academically rigorous routines and prompts follow second grade level priority standards and include whole group, individual, and partner work. The book can be used with any math program, or for small groups, workstations, or homework.

Inside you will find:

♦ 40 weeks of practice
♦ 1 activity a day
♦ 200 activities total
♦ Answer Key

For each week, the Anchor Routines cover these key areas: Monday: Reasoning; Tuesday: Vocabulary; Wednesday: Place Value; Thursday: Fluency; and Friday: Problem Solving. Get your students' math muscles moving with the easy-to-follow routines in this book!

Dr. Nicki Newton has been an educator for 30 years, working both nationally and internationally with students of all ages. She has worked on developing Math Workshop and Guided Math Institutes around the country; visit her website at www.drnickinewton.com. She is also an avid blogger (www.guidedmath.wordpress.com), tweeter (@drnickimath) and Pinterest pinner (www.pinterest.com/drnicki7).

T0346805

Day-by-Day Math Thinking Routines in Second Grade

40 Weeks of Quick Prompts and Activities

Dr. Nicki Newton

Routledge
Taylor & Francis Group

NEW YORK AND LONDON

First published 2020
by Routledge
605 Third Avenue, New York, NY 10017

and by Routledge
2 Park Square, Milton Park, Abingdon, Oxon, OX14 4RN

Routledge is an imprint of the Taylor & Francis Group, an informa business

© 2020 Taylor & Francis

Library of Congress Cataloging-in-Publication Data
Names: Newton, Nicki, author.
Title: Day-by-day math thinking routines in second grade : 40 weeks of
    quick prompts and activities / Dr. Nicki Newton.
Description: New York, NY : Routledge, 2020.
Identifiers: LCCN 2019036240 (print) | LCCN 2019036241 (ebook) | ISBN
    9780367421250 (hardback) | ISBN 9780367421243 (paperback) | ISBN
    9780367821968 (ebook)
Subjects: LCSH: Mathematics--Study and teaching (Elementary)--Activity
    programs. | Second grade (Education)
Classification: LCC QA135.6 .N4847 2020 (print) | LCC QA135.6 (ebook) |
    DDC 372.7/049--dc23
LC record available at https://lccn.loc.gov/2019036240
LC ebook record available at https://lccn.loc.gov/2019036241

ISBN: 978-0-367-42125-0 (hbk)
ISBN: 978-0-367-42124-3 (pbk)
ISBN: 978-0-367-82196-8 (ebk)

Typeset in Palatino
by Swales & Willis, Exeter, Devon, UK

Contents

Meet the Author

Dr. Nicki Newton has been an educator for 30 years, working both nationally and internationally, with students of all ages. Having spent the first part of her career as a literacy and social studies specialist, she built on those frameworks to inform her math work. She believes that math is intricately intertwined with reading, writing, listening and speaking. She has worked on developing Math Workshop and Guided Math Institutes around the country. Most recently, she has been helping districts and schools nationwide to integrate their State Standards for Mathematics and think deeply about how to teach these within a Math Workshop model. Dr. Nicki works with teachers, coaches and administrators to make math come alive by considering the powerful impact of building a community of mathematicians who make meaning of real math together. When students do real math, they learn it. They own it, they understand it, and they can do it. Every one of them. Dr. Nicki is also an avid blogger (www.guidedmath.word-press. com) and Pinterest pinner (https://www.pinterest.com/drnicki7/).

Introduction

Welcome to this exciting new series of daily math thinking routines. I have been doing thinking routines for years. People ask me all the time if I have these written down somewhere. So, I wrote a book. Now, that has turned into a grade level series so that people can do them with prompts that address their grade level standards. This is the anti-worksheet workbook!

The goal is to get students reflecting on their thinking and communicating their mathematical thinking with partners and the whole class about the math they are learning. Marzano (2007)[1] notes that

> initial understanding, albeit a good one, does not suffice for learning that is aimed at long-term retention and use of knowledge. Rather, students must have opportunities to practice new skills and deepen their understanding of new information. Without this type of extended processing, knowledge that students initially understand might fade and be lost over time.

The daily math thinking routines in this book focus on taking Depth of Knowledge activity level 1 activities, to DOK level 2 and 3 activities. Many of the questions are open. For example, we turn the traditional fluency question on it's head. Instead of asking students "What is the answer to 10 − 8?", we ask students to tell us a word problem where the answer is 2. Inspired by Marion Small (2009)[2], we don't just ask what comes after 51; we ask "What is a number that is near 51?", "What is a number that is far from 51?".

In this series, we mainly work on priority standards, although we do address some of the supporting and additional standards. This book is not intended to cover every standard. Rather, it is meant to provide ongoing daily review of the foundational ideas in math. There is a focus for each day of the week.

♦ Monday: General Thinking Routines
♦ Tuesday: Vocabulary
♦ Wednesday: Place Value
♦ Thursday: Fluency (American and British Number Talks, Number Strings)
♦ Friday: Problem Solving

There are general daily thinking routines (What Doesn't Belong?, True or False?, Convince Me), that review various priority standards from the different domains (Geometry, Algebraic Thinking, Counting, Measurement, Number Sense). Every Tuesday there is an emphasis on Vocabulary because math is a language and if you don't know the words then you can't speak it. There is a continuous review of foundational words through different games (Tic Tac Toe, Match, Bingo), because students need at least 6 encounters with a word to own it. On Wednesday there is often an emphasis on Place Value. Thursday is always some sort of fluency routine (American or British Number Talks and Number Strings). Finally, Fridays are Problem Solving routines.

The book starts with a review of priority and other kindergarten standards and then as the weeks progress the current grade level standards are integrated throughout. There is a heavy

1 Marzano, R. J. (2007). *The art and science of teaching: A comprehensive framework for effective instruction*. ASCD: Virginia.
2 Small, M. (2009). *Good Questions: Great ways to differentiate mathematics instruction*. Teachers College Press: New York.

emphasis on work within 10 and place value within 120. There is also an emphasis on geometry concepts and some data and measurement. The word problem types for second grade have been woven throughout the year.

Throughout the book there is an emphasis on the mathematical practices/processes (SMP, 2010[3]; NCTM, 2000[4]). Students are expected to problem solve in different ways. They are expected to reason by contextualizing and decontextualizing numbers. They are expected to communicate their thinking to partners and the whole group using precise mathematical vocabulary. Part of this is reading the work of others, listening to others explanations, writing about their work and then speaking about their work and the work of others in respectful ways. Students are expected to model their thinking with tools and templates. Students are continuously asked to think about the pattern and structure of numbers as they work through the activities.

These activities focus on building mathematical proficiency as defined by the NAP 2001[5]. These activities focus on conceptual understanding, procedural fluency, adaptive reasoning, strategic competence and a student's mathematical disposition. This book can be used with any math program. These are jump starters to the day. They are getting the math muscle moving at the beginning of the day.

Math routines are a form of "guided practice." Marzano notes that although the:

> guided practice is the place where students—working alone, with other students, or with the teacher—engage in the cognitive processing activities of organizing, reviewing, rehearsing, summarizing, comparing, and contrasting. However, it is important that all students engage in these activities. (p. 7)

These are engaging, standards-based, academically rigorous activities that provide meaningful routines that develop mathematical proficiency. The work can also be used for practice with in small groups, workstations and also sent home home as questions for homework.

We have focused on coherence from grade to grade, rigor of thinking, and focus on understanding and being able to explain the math the students are doing. We have intended to take deeper dives into the math, not rushing to the topics of the next grade but going deeper into the topics of the grade at hand (see Figures 1.1–1.4). Here is our criteria for selecting the routines:

◆ Engaging
◆ Easy to learn
◆ Repeatable
◆ Open-ended
◆ Easy to differentiate (adapt and extend for different levels).

3 The Standards of Mathematical Practice. "Common Core State Standards for Mathematical Practice." Washington, D.C.: National Governors Association Center for Best Practices, Council of Chief State School Officers, 2010. Retrieved on December 1, 2019 from: www.corestandards.org/Math/Practice.
4 National Council of Teachers of Mathematics. (2000). *Principles and standards for school mathematics*. Reston, VA: National Council of Teachers of Mathematics.
5 Kilpatrick, J., Swafford, J., and Findell, B. (eds.) (2001). *Adding it up: Helping children learn mathematics*. Washington, DC: National Academy Press.

Figure 1.1 Talking about the Routine!

Monday: Reasoning

3 + ___ = 7

Jen said that the answer is 10. Kelly said the answer is 4. Who do you agree with? Why?

Tuesday: Vocabulary

difference	subtract
addend	take away

Wednesday: Guess My Number

I am a 2-digit number.
I am more than 12.
I am less than 20.
My digits add up to 9.
Who am I?

Thursday: Number Strings

7 + 4
7 + 5
7 + 6
7 + 7

Friday: Make Your Own Problem

Mike had _____ marbles. He gave _____ away. How many did he have left?
    (4 or 5)   (1, 2 or 3)

Figure 1.2 The Math Routine Cycle of Engagement

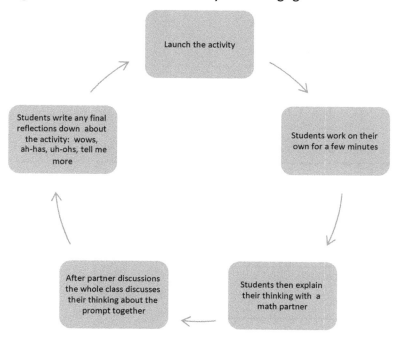

Step 1: Students are given the launch prompt. The teacher explains the prompt and makes sure that everyone understands what they are working on.

Step 2: They are given a few minutes to work on that prompt by themselves.

Step 3: The next step is for students to work with a math partner. As they work with this partner, students are expected to listen to what their partner did as well as explain their own work.

Step 4: Students come back together as a whole group and discuss the math. They are encouraged to talk about how they solved it and the similarities and differences between their thinking and their partner's thinking.

Step 5: Students reflect on the prompt of the day, thinking about what wowed them, what made them say ah-ha, what made them say uh-oh, what made them say, "I need to know more about this."

Thinking Activities

These are carefully planned practice activities to get students to think. They are **not meant to be used as a workbook**. This is a thinking activity book. The emphasis is on students doing their own work, explaining what they did with a partner and then sharing out to the entire class.

Overview of the Routines

Monday Routines – General Review (Algebraic Thinking, Measurement, Data, Geometry)

- Alike and Different
- Always, Sometimes, Never
- Convince Me!
- Graphs
- How Many More to
- It Is/It Isn't
- Magic Square
- Missing Numbers
- Number Bond It!
- Reasoning Matrices
- Venn Diagram
- 3 Truths and a Fib
- Tic Tac Toe
- True or False?
- Two Arguments
- What Doesn't Belong?

Tuesday Routines - Vocabulary

- Always, Sometimes, Never
- Frayer Model
- Find and Fix the Error
- It Is/It Isn't
- Vocabulary Bingo
- Vocabulary Brainstorm
- Vocabulary Draw
- Vocabulary Fill-in
- Vocabulary Match
- Vocabulary 1-Minute Essay/Quick Write
- Vocabulary Talk
- Vocabulary Tic Tac Toe
- What Doesn't Belong?

Wednesday Routines - Place Value

- Compose It!
- Convince Me!
- Find and Fix the Error
- Fraction of the Day
- Greater Than, Less Than, in Between
- Guess My Number
- Missing Numbers in a Hundred Grid
- How Many More to
- It Is/It Isn't
- Money Problems

- Number Bond It!
- Number Line It!
- Number of the Day
- Skip Counting
- 3 Truths and a Fib
- What Doesn't Belong?
- Why Is It Not?

Thursday Routines - Number Talks

- Number Talks
- Number Strings

Friday Routines – Problem Solving

- Equation Match
- Make Your Own Problem
- Model It
- Picture That!
- What's the Problem?
- What's the Story?
- What's the Question?
- Word Problem Sort

Figure 1.3 Overview of the Routines

Routine	Purpose	Description
Alike and Different	Students should be able to reason about how things are alike and different.	In this routine, students have to discuss how things are alike and different using math terminology.
Always, Sometimes, Never	Students should be able to reason about mathematical statements.	Students have to discuss whether a statement is always, sometimes or never true.
Composing Numbers/ Money	Composing and decomposing numbers is a stepping stone to adding and subtracting.	Students use Ten frames to compose and decompose different numbers.
Convince Me!	This routine focuses on students reasoning about different topics. They have to convince their peers about specific statements.	Students are given different things to think about like statements or equations and they have to convince their peers that they are correct.
Equation Match	This routine focuses on students thinking about which operation they would use to solve a problem. It requires that they reason about the actions that are happening in the problem and then what they are required to do to solve the problem.	Students are trying to match the word problem and the equation.
Find and Fix the Error	Students have to reason about the problems and decide whether or not statements make sense.	In this routine, the students have to find the error in a problem and decide how to fix it.
Fraction of the Day	Students should be able to reason about fractions.	In this routine, students write about and draw benchmark fractions.
Frayer Model	This routine is meant to get students talking about concepts. They are supposed to talk about the definition, what happens in real life, sketch an example and also give non-examples.	Students are given a template with labels. They work through the template writing and drawing about the specified topic.
Graphs	Students should know how to read and interpret data.	Students have to read the information and then make a graph based on that information and ask questions about the information.

Routine	Purpose	Description
Guess My Number	This routine gives students a variety of clues about a number and asks the students to guess which number it might be given all the clues. Students have to use their understanding of place value and math vocabulary to figure out which number is being discussed.	In this routine, students are given various clues about a number and they must use the clues to guess which number it is.
How Many More to	In this routine, students are asked to tell how many to a specific number. Again, this is another place value routine, asking students to reason about numbers on the number line.	In this routine, students are given a specific number and they have to tell how many more to another designated number.
It Is/It Isn't	This routine can be used in a variety of ways. Students have to look at the topic and decide what it is and what it isn't. It is another way of looking at example, non-example.	In this routine, students discuss what something is and what it isn't.
Legs and Feet	Legs and feet is a great arithmetic routine which gets students to use various operations to figure out how many animals there are by working with numbers.	Students look at different animals and think about how many legs and feet there could be given that number of animals.
Magic Square	In this routine, students are working on basic facts of addition and subtraction.	They are given the sum of the magic square that must work in all directions and then they have to figure out what to put in the space to make that sum.
Make Your Own Problem	In this word problem routine students get to pick their own numbers to create and then solve a word problem.	Students fill in the blanks with numbers to make their own problems.
Missing Numbers	Students should be able to reason about equations.	Students fill in missing numbers in an equation.
Missing Numbers in a Hundred Grid	Students should understand and use place value to fill in the number grid.	Students have to figure out what is missing in the empty squares of a hundred grid.
Model It	In this word problem routine, students are focusing on representing word problems in a variety of ways.	Students have to represent their thinking about a word problem with various models.

Routine	Purpose	Description
Number Bond It!	In this routine, students are working on decomposing numbers in a variety of ways.	Students use number bonds to break apart numbers in different ways.
Number of the Day	This activity focuses on students modeling numbers in a variety of ways.	This activity has a given number and students have to represent that number in different ways.
Number Line It!	This activity focuses on sequencing numbers correctly.	Students have to put numbers in the correct sequence on the number path.
Number Talks	This activity focuses on number sense. Students compose and decompose numbers, as well as add and subtract numbers.	Students work out the different problems and discuss the various strategies they are using.
Number Strings	In this routine, students are looking at the relationship between a set of problems.	The teacher gives the students number strings around a specific concept. For example, students work on subtracting 1 and then discuss the pattern.
Reasoning Matrices	Reasoning matrices helps students to reason about information and decide what makes sense given that information.	In this routine, students are given information about children and they have to decide which information matches which child.
Venn Diagram	Students should be able to reason about the information.	In this routine, students have to set up and discuss information in a Venn diagram. They must decide what fits in which categories.
Skip Counting	Students should be able to skip count.	In this routine, students have to reason about the pattern and decide what comes next.
3 Truths and a Fib	Students should reason about mathematical statements.	In this routine, students are given 4 statements. Three statements are true and one is false. Students have to decide which one is false.
True or False?	This activity focuses on students reasoning about what is true or false.	Students are given different things to think about like statements about shapes or equations and they have to state and prove whether they are true or false.
2 Arguments	In this reasoning routine, students are thinking about common errors that students make when doing various math tasks like missing numbers, working with properties and working with the equal sign.	Students listen to the way 2 different students approached a problem, decide who they agree with and defend their thinking.

Routine	Purpose	Description
Vocabulary Bingo	This activity focuses on vocabulary.	Students play Bingo. Teachers will need to make copies of the boards for students. Or the students can play it in teams as a class on the board.
Vocabulary Brainstorm	This activity focuses on vocabulary.	Students brainstorm about math vocabulary. They can brainstorm using words, pictures and numbers.
Vocabulary Draw	Students should understand and know how to use math vocabulary.	In this routine, students write and draw about math vocabulary words.
Vocabulary Match	Students should understand and know how to use math vocabulary.	In this routine, students match the vocabulary words with definitions and/or pictures.
Vocabulary Greater Than, Less Than, in Between	Students should understand the relationship of numbers to each other on the number line	Students have to discuss number relationships given specific numbers.
Vocabulary Talk	Students discuss vocabulary words.	In this activity, students discuss one or more words in a conversation.
Vocabulary Tic Tac Toe	Students should be able to name and use math vocabulary.	Students have to discuss the words with their partner. They have to draw or write or explain their thinking before they put the x or o. Whoever gets 3 in a row first wins. Teachers will need to make copies of the boards for students. Or the students can play it in teams as a class on the board.
Vocabulary Fill-in	Students focus on vocabulary.	Students read the sentences and fill in the missing words.
Vocabulary Quick Write	Students need to know math vocabulary.	In this activity they write down everything they can about a given word. They can use numbers, words and pictures.
What Doesn't Belong?	This is a reasoning activity where students have to choose which objects they can group together and why. The emphasis is on justification.	Students have 4 squares. They have to figure out which object does not belong.
What's the Story?/Picture That!	Students should be able to tell a story when given objects or a picture.	In this routine, students are shown a picture and they have to tell what is happening in the story.

Routine	Purpose	Description
What's the Problem?	Students should be able to contextualize numbers.	In this routine, students are given an equation and they have to choose the problem that matches the equation.
What's the Question?	Students should be able to reason about a story context.	Students are given a story context and they have to come up with questions about that context.
Why Is It Not?	Students reason about math errors.	In this routine, students have to reason and explain why the wrong answer is incorrect.
Word Problem Sort	Students should be able to reason about problems and decide what type of problem they are looking at.	In this routine, students have to sort addition and subtraction problems.

Questioning Is the Key 🔑

To Unlock the Magic of Thinking, You Need Good Questions!

Figure 1.4

Launch Questions (before the activity)	Process Questions (during the activity)
◆ What is this prompt asking us to do? ◆ How will you start? ◆ What are you thinking? ◆ Explain to your math partner, your understanding of the question. ◆ What will you do to solve this problem?	◆ What will you do first? ◆ How will you organize your thinking? ◆ What might you do to get started? ◆ What is your strategy? ◆ Why did you…? ◆ Why are you doing that? ◆ Is that working? Does it make sense? ◆ Is that a reasonable answer? ◆ Can you prove it? ◆ Are you sure about that answer? ◆ How do you know you are correct?
Debrief Questions (after the activity)	**Partner Questions (guide student conversations)**
◆ What did you do? ◆ How did you get your answer? ◆ How do you know it is correct? ◆ Can you prove it? ◆ Convince me that you have the correct answer. ◆ Is there another way to think about this problem?	◆ Tell me what you did. ◆ Tell me more about your model. ◆ Tell me more about your drawing. ◆ Tell me more about your calculations. ◆ Tell me more about your thinking. ◆ Can you prove it? ◆ How do you know you are right? ◆ I understand what you did. ◆ I don't understand what you did yet.

Daily Routines

Monday: What Doesn't Belong?

In this routine students have to discuss what 3 of the following numbers, letters, shapes and images belong together. They have to eliminate the one that does not go with the others.

Tuesday: Vocabulary Match

Students have to match the word with the description.

Wednesday: Convince Me!

Students have to look at the problem and prove that it is true with the number grid and the number line.

Thursday: Number Talk

This is an opportunity for students to work on talking about addition of numbers. The focus should be on different strategies such as bridging ten, doubles plus two or doubles minus two.

Friday: What's the Question?

Read together out loud with your class 3 times.

1st time: Think about what the story is about.

2nd time: Think about what the numbers mean.

3rd time: Come up with some questions about the story and answer them.

Students read the scenario and they have to come up with 2 questions that are appropriate for the scenario.

Monday: What Doesn't Belong?

Find the one that does not belong in each set.

A.

7 + 3	11 − 1
8 + 4	3 + 2 + 5

B.

5 − 2	6 − 3
7 − 5	1 + 1 + 1

Tuesday: Vocabulary Match

Match the word and the definition.

sum	the symbol used for subtraction
addend	the answer to an addition problem
minus sign	one of the numbers in an addition equation
difference	the answer to a subtraction problem

Wednesday: Convince Me!

Prove it with numbers, words and/or pictures!

$50 - 10 = 40$

1	2	3	4	5	6	7	8	9	10
11	12	13	14	15	16	17	18	19	20
21	22	23	24	25	26	27	28	29	30
31	32	33	34	35	36	37	38	39	40
41	42	43	44	45	46	47	48	49	50
51	52	53	54	55	56	57	58	59	60
61	62	63	64	65	66	67	68	69	70
71	72	73	74	75	76	77	78	79	80
81	82	83	84	85	86	87	88	89	90
91	92	93	94	95	96	97	98	99	100

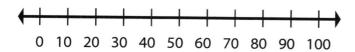

0 10 20 30 40 50 60 70 80 90 100

Thursday: Number Talk

What are some ways to think about:

$$7 + 5$$

Friday: What's the Question?

Read together out loud with your class 3 times.
1st time: Think about what the story is about.
2nd time: Think about what the numbers mean.
3rd time: Come up with some questions about the story and answer them.

Think of at least 2 questions you could ask about this story. Write them down. Discuss with your classmates.

Mary has 2 red marbles, 3 blue marbles and 5 pink ones.
1)

2)

Week 2 Teacher Notes

Monday: Magic Square

In a magic square the students have to add up, down, across, and diagonally to find the magic number.

Tuesday: Vocabulary Tic Tac Toe

Students play Tic Tac Toe with a math partner. They pick a square and write or draw what the word means. Whoever gets 3 in a row wins.

At the end of the game, go over the possible answers with the entire class. Have students discuss what they wrote as answers.

Wednesday: Number Line It!

Students have to discuss how to order and plot the numbers on the number line from least to greatest.

Thursday: Number Talk

Students work on adding the numbers and discussing their strategies. They have to pick a number from each circle and then discuss whether or not they did it in their head, with numbers or used a model.

Friday: What's the Problem?

The answer was 5 toy trucks. What was the question?

Story

Model

Equation

Monday: Magic Squares

Find the magic number by adding up, down, across, and diagonally.

Tuesday: Vocabulary Tic Tac Toe

Play tic tac toe with a math partner. Pick a square and write or draw what the word means. Whoever gets 3 in a row wins.

Game 1

sum	addend	subtract
plus sign	minus sign	difference
total	altogether	add

Game 2 Name the shape.

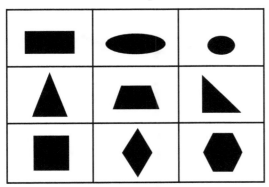

Wednesday: Number Line It!

Place these numbers on the number line.

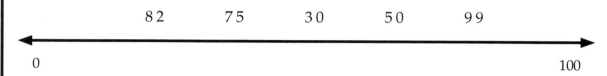

82   75   30   50   99

0   100

Compare your response with your partner. Explain your thinking. How do you know you are correct?

Thursday: Number Talk

Pick a number from each circle. Decide how you are going to solve it. Write the problem under the way you solved it. For example, 8 + 2. I can do that in my head because it is a ten friend.

Did I do it in my head?	Did I use a model?	Did I write down the numbers and solve it on paper?

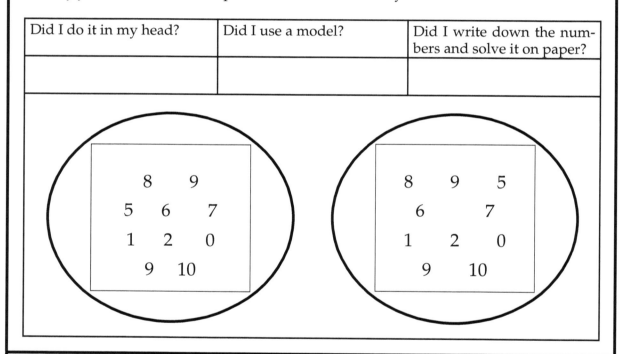

Friday: What's the Problem?

Put a line under the take away problems. Put a circle around the join problems. Answer all of the problems.

1. Sue had 5 rings. She got some more. Now she has 10. How many rings did she get?

2. Luke had 10 cards. He gave 5 away. How many cards does he have now?

3. Marco had 7 marbles. He gave some to his brother. Now he has 5. How many marbles did he give away?

4. Maria had 8 bracelets. She got some more. Now she has 10. How many bracelets did she get?

Monday: Always, Sometimes, Never

Students read the statement and discuss and then decide if it is always, sometimes or never true.

Tuesday: It Is/It Isn't

Students have to discuss what a hexagon is and is not.

Wednesday: Number of the Day

Students have to fill in the boxes to represent the number twenty. Have the students do it on their own, discuss with a partner and then debrief whole class.

Thursday: Number Strings

Students work on solving the problem in different ways.

Friday: Model That!

Students have to model the expression on a number line, twenty frame and by doing a math sketch.

Week 3 Activities

Monday: Always, Sometimes, Never

Read the statement and decide if it is always, sometimes or never true.

When you add 2 numbers, the number always gets bigger.

Tuesday: It Is/It Isn't

Discuss what a hexagon is and is not.

Hexagon

It Is	It Isn't

Word bank: Straight lines, curved lines, vertices, angles, polygon.

Wednesday: Number of the Day

Fill in the boxes using the number 10.

10

Number word.	Show 2 addition sentences that make ten.
Show 2 subtraction sentences that make ten.	Add 3 numbers that make ten.

Thursday: Number Strings

What are some ways to think about and show:

1st Talk	2nd Talk
7 + 7	17 + 5
7 + 6	17 + 6
7 + 5	17 + 7
7 + 4	17 + 8

Friday: Model That!

Model the problem in different ways.

$$7 + 8$$

Number Line

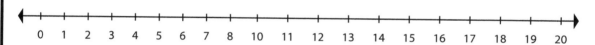

Double Ten Frame

Math Sketch

Week 4 Teacher Notes

Monday: Find and Fix the Error

Students have to discuss and decide who is correct. They need to defend their thinking with a partner. This is an opportunity to discuss the meaning of the equal sign.

Tuesday: Frayer Model

Students have to use the frayer model as a frame to discuss a rectangle.

Wednesday: Greater Than, Less Than, in Between

Students have to reason about numbers on their mental number line.

Thursday: Number Talk

Students discuss ways to do this subtraction problem. The emphasis is on talking about the strategies.

Friday: Picture That!

Students have to tell a story about the pictures. They can tell an addition or subtraction story. They should write a number sentence as well.

Week 4 Activities

Monday: Find and Fix the Error

Find the error below and fix it. Discuss with your math partner.

Mike said that 6 + ___ = 8 is 14. He is incorrect. Explain to your partner why. Be ready to share your thinking with the whole group.

Tuesday: Frayer Model

Fill in the boxes using the word.

Rectangle

It is	It is not
2 different ways it could look	In real life we see them…

Wednesday: Greater Than, Less Than, in Between

Fill in the boxes using the numbers.

15   50   90

Name a number greater than 15.	Name a number greater than 90.	Name a number greater than 20 less than 50.
Name a number less than 90.	Name a number in between 15 and 90.	Name a number in between 15 and 50.

Thursday: Number Talk

What are some ways to subtract 14 – 6?

Friday: Picture That!

Tell a story about the animals.

Story:

Number sentence:

Week 5 Teacher Notes

Monday: 2 Arguments

In this routine the students discuss which student is correct.

Tuesday: Vocabulary Match

Students have to match the word with the correct definition by drawing lines from the definition to the correct example.

Wednesday: Missing Numbers in a Hundred Grid

Students decide which numbers are missing in the spaces by using place value.

Thursday: Number Talk

Students pick a number from each circle. They then discuss which strategy they used to solve the problem, either mental math, a model or computation with the numbers on paper.

Friday: Make Your Own Problem

Students have to fill in the numbers and discuss the problem.

Week 5 Activities

Monday: 2 Arguments

Read the 2 arguments. Decide who you agree with. Discuss with a partner.

$$8 - \underline{\hspace{1cm}} = 4$$

John said the answer was 12.

Maria said the answer was 4.

Who do you agree with?

Why?

Tuesday: Vocabulary Match

Match the word and the shape.

circle

square

rectangle

hexagon

trapezoid

triangle

Wednesday: Missing Numbers in a Hundred Grid

Fill in the missing numbers on the hundred grid.

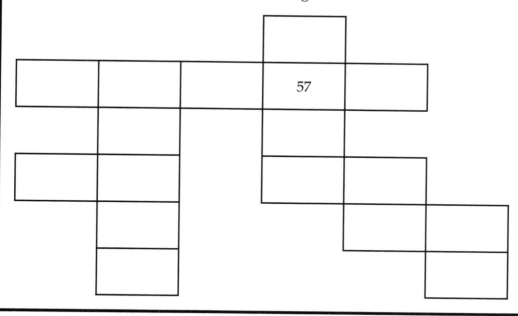

Thursday: Number Talk

Pick a number from each circle. Add them. Then, decide how you are going to solve it. Write the problem under the way you solved it. For example, 8 + 2. I can do that in my head because it is a ten friend.

Did I do it in my head?	Did I use a model?	Did I write down the numbers and solve it on paper?

18   19
15   16   8
17   9   11
20   10   7
9   10

8   9   5
6   4
7   1   2
0

Friday: Make Your Own Problem

Make your own problem by filling in the blanks.

Ray had _____ marbles. He got _____ more for his birthday. Now, he has _____.

Model it!

Number sentence (equation): _____

Monday: Alike and Different

Students should be able to discuss how the shapes are alike with sides that are closed, how they have points (vertices) and how the sides are straight. We want to focus on the attributes of the shapes.

Tuesday: Vocabulary 1-Minute Essay

Students write down everything they can about addition. They can use numbers, words and pictures. They then switch and add to their math partner's page with more ideas. Then, they switch back and add 1 more thing.

Wednesday: How Many More to

Students have to reason about numbers. They need to know how many more to a given number.

Thursday: Number Strings

In this number talk, students talk about adding 4 to a number. They look at and discuss the pattern.

Friday: Equation Match

Students have to match the problem with the appropriate equation.

Week 6 Activities

Monday: Alike and Different

Discuss how these shapes are alike and different.

Square and Hexagon

Alike	Different

Word bank: straight sides, vertices, polygons, angles, closed sides.

Tuesday: Vocabulary 1-Minute Essay

(For 30 seconds) Write everything you can about addition. Use numbers words and pictures.

(15 seconds) Now switch with a neighbor and add 1 thing to their list.

(15 seconds) Now add 1 more thing to your list.

Wednesday: How Many More to

Start at 56. How many more to 70?

Start at 89. How many more to 100?

Start at 34. How many more to 50?

1	2	3	4	5	6	7	8	9	10
11	12	13	14	15	16	17	18	19	20
21	22	23	24	25	26	27	28	29	30
31	32	33	34	35	36	37	38	39	40
41	42	43	44	45	46	47	48	49	50
51	52	53	54	55	56	57	58	59	60
61	62	63	64	65	66	67	68	69	70
71	72	73	74	75	76	77	78	79	80
81	82	83	84	85	86	87	88	89	90
90	91	92	93	94	95	96	97	99	100

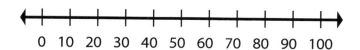

0 10 20 30 40 50 60 70 80 90 100

Thursday: Number Strings

What are some ways to think about and show:

$$9 + 4$$
$$19 + 4$$
$$29 + 4$$
$$59 + 4$$
$$79 + 4$$

Friday: Equation Match

Match the story with the equation.

Jan had 5 lollipops. She got some more. Now she has 10. How many lollipops did she get?

A. $5 + 10 = \square$
B. $5 + \square = 10$
C. $10 + \square = 5$
D. Equation is not here.

Week 7 Teacher Notes

Monday: 2 Arguments

Students have to read and discuss the problem. They need to decide who they agree with and then defend their thinking with numbers, words and pictures.

Tuesday: Vocabulary Brainstorm

Students write about the word using numbers, words and pictures.

Wednesday: Guess My Number

Students have to read the clues and figure out, through a process of elimination, what the number is.

Thursday: Number Talk

Students have to discuss adding 15 and 7. They should explore different strategies and talk about what is efficient.

Friday: Equation Match

Students have to match the equation with the correct problem.

Monday: 2 Arguments

Read the 2 arguments. Decide who you agree with. Discuss with a partner.

Jessica said that $4 + 3 = 7 - 0$ cannot be true because one side is addition and the other side is subtraction. Marvin said it doesn't matter. The important thing is to look and see if both sides equal the same number.

Who do you agree with?

Why?

Prove it!

Tuesday: Vocabulary Brainstorm

In each thought cloud write or draw something that has to do with subtraction.

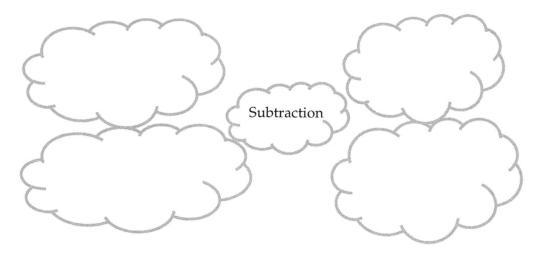

Subtraction

Wednesday: Guess My Number

Use the clues to guess the number.

A.	B.
My number is greater than 5.	My number is greater than 20.
My number is less than 10.	My number is less than 25.
My number is not odd.	My number is not even.
My number is less than 5 + 2.	My number is less than 25 - 3.
What is my number?	What is my number?

← 1 2 3 4 5 6 7 8 9 10 11 12 13 14 15 16 17 18 19 20 21 22 23 24 25 26 27 28 29 30 →

Thursday: Number Talk

What are some ways to add 15 + 7?

Friday: Equation Match

Match the equation to the correct story.

$$10 - \square = 7$$

Problem A	Problem B
Kelly had 10 marbles. She got 7 more. How many does she have now?	Kelly had 10 marbles. She gave some away and now she has 7. How many did she give away?

Monday: True or False?

In this routine the students discuss whether or not this figure is a hexagon. They should reason out loud.

Tuesday: Vocabulary Tic Tac Toe

Students play rock, paper, scissors to see who starts the game. They take turns picking squares. Before they can mark it with an x or o they have to write the definition or draw a picture of the item in the square. Whoever gets 3 in a row first, wins.

At the end of the game, go over the possible answers with the entire class. Have students discuss what they wrote as answers.

Wednesday: Number Bond It!

This is an opportunity for students to build on their work on composing and decomposing numbers to 14.

Thursday: Number Talk

This is an opportunity for students to work on subtraction within 20. They have to pick 1 number from each circle and then make a problem and discuss how they solved it.

Friday: What's the Problem?

Students work on representing word problems with a tape/strip diagram.

Monday: True or False?

Decide whether the statement is true or false. Discuss with a partner.

This is a hexagon.

1. Think about it.
2. Share your thinking with a friend. Defend your answer.
3. Share your thinking with the group.

Tuesday: Vocabulary Tic Tac Toe

Play rock, paper, scissors to see who starts the game. Take turns picking squares. Before you mark it with an x or o you have to write the definition or draw a picture of the item in the square. Whoever gets 3 in a row first, wins.

addend	subtract	hundreds
equal	tens	digit
equation	octagon	ones

fewer	greater	same
more	less	compare
expanded form	pentagon	triangle

Wednesday: Number Bond It!

Show how to break apart 14 in 3 different ways!

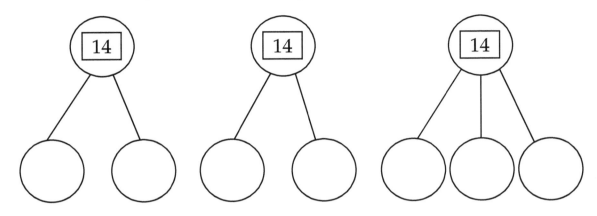

Thursday: Number Talk

Pick a number from each circle. Make a subtraction problem. Write the problem under the way you solved it. For example, 18 – 9, I can do that in my head because it is a half fact.

Did I do it in my head?	Did I use a model?	Did I write down the numbers and solve it on paper?

A.

18	11	15	8
14	9	13	12
10	7		

B.

8	9	5
6	4	7
1	2	0
9	10	

Friday: What's the Problem?

Model that! Read the problem and model it with a tape diagram.

Jamal had 7 marbles. He had 2 more than Mike. How many did Mike have?

Monday: Convince Me!

Students reason about why the equation is true. They can prove it with numbers, words and pictures.

Tuesday: It Is/It Isn't

Students discuss the word pentagon.

Wednesday: Skip Counting

Students work on skip counting by 2s in a variety of ways.

Thursday: Number Strings

Students discuss what the pattern is that they see in these expressions. The discussion should focus on what happens when they take away 8 or 9 from a number.

Friday: What's the Question?

Students work on telling and representing word problems in different ways.

Week 9 Activities

Monday: Convince Me!

Convince me that:
$$4 + 6 + 2 = 10 + 2$$

Tuesday: It Is/It Isn't

Decide and discuss what a pentagon is and is not.

Pentagon

It Is	It Isn't

Word bank: Polygon, straight, sides, angles, vertices, shape, square, figure, closed, open.

Wednesday: Skip Counting

Name 2 numbers less than 20 that you would say if you were skip counting by 2s.

Name 2 numbers greater than 50 that you would say if you were skip counting by 2s.

Name 2 numbers greater than 100 that you would say if you were skip counting by 2s.

Thursday: Number Strings

What are some ways to think about and show:

$$12 - 9$$
$$22 - 9$$
$$42 - 8$$
$$62 - 8$$
$$73 - 9$$
$$84 - 9$$

Friday: What's the Question?

The answer is 10 stickers. What is the question?

1	2	3	4	5	6	7	8	9	10
11	12	13	14	15	16	17	18	19	20
21	22	23	24	25	26	27	28	29	30
31	32	33	34	35	36	37	38	39	40
41	42	43	44	45	46	47	48	49	50
51	52	53	54	55	56	57	58	59	60
61	62	63	64	65	66	67	68	69	70
71	72	73	74	75	76	77	78	79	80
81	82	83	84	85	86	87	88	89	90
91	92	93	94	95	96	97	98	99	100

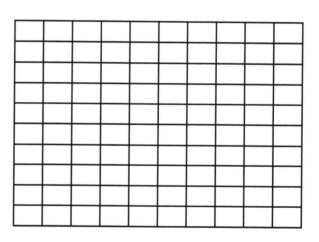

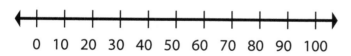

0 10 20 30 40 50 60 70 80 90 100

Week 10 Teacher Notes

Monday: Reasoning Matrix

Students have to read the clues and decide which pie each child ate.

Tuesday: Vocabulary Tic Tac Toe

Students play Tic Tac Toe. Before they can pick a square they have to write the definition or draw a picture of the item in the square. Whoever gets 3 in a row first, wins.

At the end of the game, go over the possible answers with the entire class. Have students discuss what they wrote as answers.

Wednesday: Number of the Day

Students have to fill in the boxes to represent the number 47. Have the students do it on their own, discuss with a partner and then debrief whole class.

Thursday: Number Talk

The focus of this conversation should be on different strategies for adding 2 2-digit numbers.

Friday: What's the Story?

Students have to tell a story about these marbles.

Monday: Reasoning Matrix

Use the clues to figure out who ate which pie. Jenny does not like fruit. Jamal loves nuts. Miguel loves fruit and hates chocolate. Kelly loves lemony-tasting things.

	Lemon pie	Strawberry pie	Chocolate pie	Pecan pie
Jenny				
Jamal				
Miguel				
Kelly				

Tuesday: Vocabulary Tic Tac Toe

Play rock, paper, scissors to see who starts the game. Take turns picking squares. Before you mark it with an x or o you have to write the definition or draw a picture of the item in the square. Whoever gets 3 in a row first, wins.

A.

<	+	greater than
>	−	less than
fewer	=	more

B.

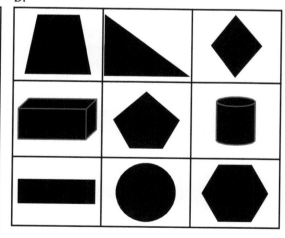

Wednesday: Number of the Day

Fill in the boxes based on the number.

47

Word form	10 more	10 less
Expanded form	_____ + _____ = 47	_____ − _____ = 47
Base ten sketch	How many more to 100?	Odd or even?

Thursday: Number Talk

What are some ways to add 45 + 17?

Friday: What's the Story?

Tell a word problem about these marbles.

	Use these questions to think about your story:
	Is it a join story or a take away story?
	What is the equation?
	What is the solution?

Week 11 Teacher Notes

Monday: Reasoning

Students have to reason about the information given to them and then decide on the categories. Then they decide which child matches the descriptions.

Tuesday: What Doesn't Belong?

Students have to decide which word doesn't go with the others.

Wednesday: What's Missing?

Students look at and discuss the missing numbers. They should use the language of patterning, such as increasing, decreasing, skip counting, etc.

Thursday: Number Talk

Students practice making double-digit addition problems within 100. They have to discuss how they solved them.

Friday: What's the Question?

Students read the scenario and then come up with several questions related to it.

Monday: Reasoning

Look at the pictures. Decide what the two different categories are. Decide how some things from each category are the same.

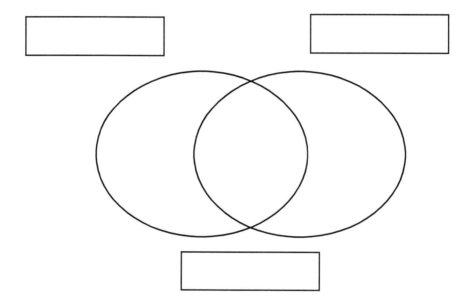

Tuesday: What Doesn't Belong?

Choose the one that does not belong to each set. Discuss with a partner.

A.

plus sign	minus sign
equal sign	clock

B.

▬	●
▲	■

Wednesday: What's Missing?

Look at the pattern and fill in the missing number.

25, _____, _____, 55, 65, 75 _____

_____, _____, 96, _____, _____, 102, 104

_____. _____., _____, _____90, _____, 110, _____, 130

Make your own pattern below.

_____, _____, _____, _____, _____, _____, _____

Thursday: Number Talk

Pick a number from each circle. Make an addition problem. Write the problem under the way you solved it. For example, 40 + 20. I can do that in my head because I just count up by 10s.

Did I do it in my head?	Did I use a model?	Did I write down the numbers and solve it on paper?

A.

```
    35      40
  61      79
  89  99     22
  54   100    77
```

B.

```
   8    9    5
      6  4
   7    1    20
   0   10
```

Friday: What's the Question?

Read together out loud with your class 3 times.
1st time: Think about what the story is about.
2nd time: Think about what the numbers mean.
3rd time: Come up with some questions about the story and answer them.

The bakery had 5 lemon cookies, 3 sugar cookies and 7 chocolate chip cookies.	What are some questions that you can ask?

Week 12 Teacher Notes

Monday: Graph It

Students have to read the frequency table, make a bar graph and ask and answer 3 questions about the data.

Tuesday: Frayer Model

Students have to discuss the vocabulary using the frayer frame.

Wednesday: Compose It!

Students have to compose the number in several different ways.

Thursday: Number Talk

Students discuss a variety of ways to solve and model ways to subtract ones from a teen number.

Friday: Picture That!

Students have to make up their own problem.

Monday: Graph It

Graph the information from the Frequency table onto the bar graph.

Frequency Table	Bar Graph
Our Favorite Fruit	Our Favorite Fruit
strawberries 10	
apples 7	10 9 8 7 6 5 4 3 2 1 0
oranges 8	Apples Oranges Bananas Strawberries Other
bananas 8	
other 2	

Ask and answer 3 questions about this graph.

Tuesday: Frayer Model

Discuss the word. Fill in the boxes to describe and give examples of the word.

Measure

Definition	Examples
Real life	**Non-examples**

Wednesday: Compose It!

Use 2 different crayons (colors) to show 4 ways to make the number 12 on the models below.

Explain your thinking to a partner. Be ready to share your thinking with the whole class.

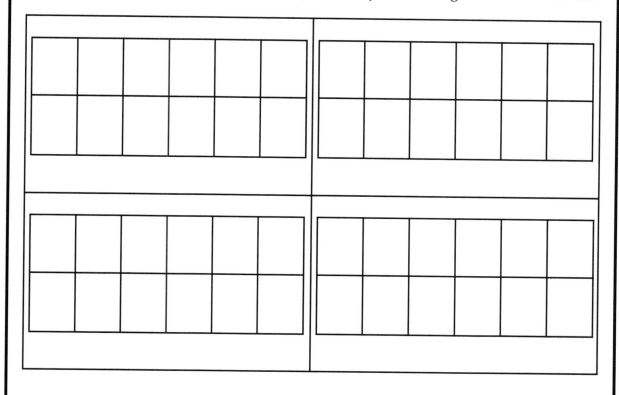

Thursday: Number Talk

What are some strategies and models to think about and show:

18 – 8
17 – 7
15 – 5
13 – 3

What do you notice about all these problems?

Friday: Picture That!

Use the picture to write a story problem.

Monday: What Doesn't Belong?

Students have to choose the one that does not belong to each set.

Tuesday: Frayer Model

Students have to discuss the word using the frayer model as a frame.

Wednesday: Legs and Feet

Students have to reason about numbers using animals.

Thursday: Number Talk

Students talk about different strategies that they could use to solve this problem. They should recognize it has a half fact and that it is related to doubles. They could also talk about how it can be done as a bridge ten fact … bridge back 4 and then 3 more.

Friday: Model That!

Students model and solve the problem.

Week 13 Activities

Monday: What Doesn't Belong?

Choose the one that does not belong to each set.

A.

add	difference
sum	join

B.

$3 + 7 + 5$	$8 + 3 + 0$
$4 + 6 + 1$	$14 - 3$

Tuesday: Frayer Model

Fill in the boxes using the word.

Equation

Definition	Examples
Give a Picture Example	Non-examples

Wednesday: Legs and Feet

Read the problems and answer them.

| A. How many legs?   | B. If there are 10 legs, how many chickens and how many crickets could you have? You have to have at least 1 of each. |

C. If there are 14 legs and there has to be a chicken and a cricket, then how many animals are there? What type could they be?

Way 1	Way 2

Thursday: Number Talk

What are some ways to think about and show:

14 − 7

Friday: Model That!

Read and model the problem.

Mary had 15 rings. She gave some to her sister. Now she has 8 left. How many did she give to her sister?

Ten Frame

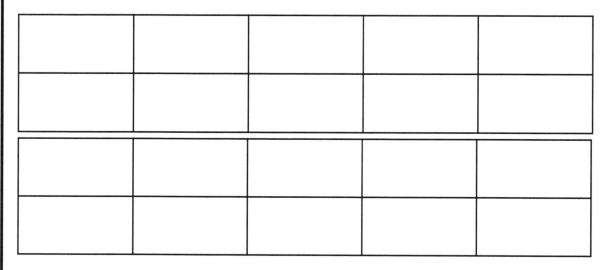

Number Line

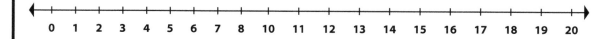

Week 14 Teacher Notes

Monday: Always, Sometimes, Never

Students have to listen to the statement and then discuss and decide if this statement is always, sometime or never true!

Tuesday: Vocabulary Bingo

Teacher will call out various attributes or names of the shapes and then students cover a shape that fits the description. They can only cover 1 shape at a time. For example: I am a shape with 4 sides or I am a shape with 3 sides or I am a hexagon.

Wednesday: Guess My Number

Students use the clues to guess the number. They can use number lines and number grids to help them.

Thursday: Number Talk

Students discuss doubles facts.

Friday: Math Story

Students work on telling and solving word problems with a variety of models.

Monday: Always, Sometimes, Never

Discuss and decide if this statement is always, sometime or never true:

Teachers are always at least 20 years older than 2nd graders.

Tuesday: Vocabulary Bingo

Pick a board. Cover 1 object at a time as your teacher names or describes it. Whoever gets 4 in a row, across, up or down or diagonally wins.

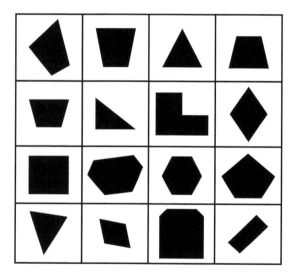 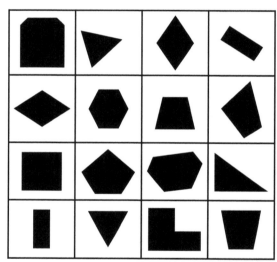

Word bank: quadrilateral, triangle, square, trapezoid, hexagon, pentagon, rhombus, rectangle.

Wednesday: Guess My Number

Use the clues to guess the number. Look at a hundred grid to help you figure out the number.

A.	B.
I am a 2-digit number. I am greater than 100. I am less than 120. If you skip count by 10's you will say my number. Who am I?	I am a 2-digit number. I am in between 25 and 33. I am an odd number. The sum of my digits is less than 5. Who am I?

Thursday: Number Talk

What are doubles plus 1 facts? How do they help us to add?

Friday: Math Story

Use the pictures and write a comparison story.

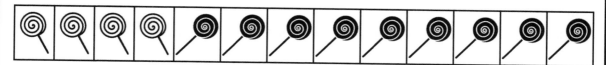

Story

Model

Equation

Week 15 Teacher Notes

Monday: How Many More to

How many more to 20? Students have to reason about numbers. They need to know how many more to a given number.

Tuesday: Vocabulary Fill-in

Students have to use the words in the word bank to fill in the blanks.

Wednesday: What Doesn't Belong?

In this routine students have to discuss what doesn't belong. They should be able to talk about what 3 of the boxes have in common and how the other one is different. There is often more than 1 thing that can be correct.

Thursday: Number Strings

Students discuss what happens when we subtract 10 from a number.

Friday: Model in the Part-Part Whole Mat

Students read and solve the problem using the diagram.

Week 15 Activities

Monday: How Many More to

Look at the number line to help you think about how many more to 20.

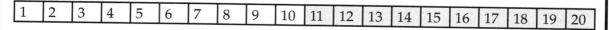

| 1 | 2 | 3 | 4 | 5 | 6 | 7 | 8 | 9 | 10 | 11 | 12 | 13 | 14 | 15 | 16 | 17 | 18 | 19 | 20 |

Start at 5…
Start at 8
Start at 9
Start at 12
Start at 17

Tuesday: Vocabulary Fill-in

Use the words in the word bank to fill in the blanks below.

Word bank: polygon, circle, hexagon, quadrilateral

A. A shape with 4 sides is called a _____.

B. A shape with 6 sides is called a _____.

C. A shape with closed, straight sides, that has angles and vertices is called a _____.

D. A shape with 1 curved side is called a _____.

Wednesday: What Doesn't Belong?

Look at the options in each box. Figure out which one doesn't belong. Decide and discuss.

A.

$14 - 7$	$12 - 6$
$18 - 9$	$10 - 4$

B.

$5 + 6$	$7 + 8$
$8 + 9$	$9 + 1$

Thursday: Number Strings

What are some ways to think about and show:

$$10 - 10$$
$$90 - 10$$
$$50 - 10$$
$$20 - 10$$
$$120 - 10$$

Friday: Model in the Part-Part Whole Mat

Read and model the problem.

Mary had 18 rings. Some were blue and 9 were red. How many were blue?

A.

Whole	
Part	Part

B. Equation (write an equation with a symbol for the part we are looking for).

Monday: Reasoning Matrices

Students have to reason about the information given to them and then decide which child matches the description.

Tuesday: Vocabulary Bingo

Students listen for their numbers and then cover 1 number at a time. Whoever gets 4 in a row, across, up or down or diagonally wins.

Wednesday: Missing Numbers

Students have to fill in the missing numbers in the hundred grid.

Thursday: Number Talk

Students work on adding numbers. They have to discuss whether or not they did it in their head, with a drawing or on paper.

Friday: Model That!

Students work on word problems using a variety of models.

Monday: Reasoning Matrices

Read the clues and decide the favorite animal of each child.

Sue and Carl like insects. Carl and Lucy like animals that hop. Sue likes caterpillars as well. Lucy likes animals that live on water and on land.			
Sue			
Carl			
Lucy			

Tuesday: Vocabulary Bingo

As your teacher calls a number, cover it. 1 number at a time.

Phrases: Cover a number greater than.
Cover a number less than. Cover a number with ___ tens.
Cover a number equal to. Cover a number with ____ ones.
Cover a number with _____ tens and _____ones.
Cover a number in between _____ and _____.
Cover a number with _____ hundreds and _____ tens and _____ ones.

A.

11	143	105	107
120	250	165	99
12	101	139	277
0	27	5	182

B.

1	134	201	172
90	45	52	75
11	109	167	88
229	100	95	0

Wednesday: Missing Numbers

Fill in the missing numbers on the hundred grid puzzle.

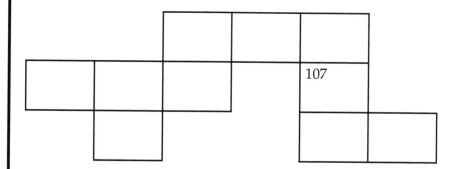

Thursday: Number Talk

Pick a number from each circle. Add them. Decide how you will solve it and write that expression under the title.

Did I do it in my head?	Did I use a model?	Did I write down the numbers and solve it on paper?

A.

52 63 74

85 96 17 38
29 41

B.

12 13 14   15

16   17   18

19   20   21

Friday: Model That!

Read the problem and model it.

There are 4 butterflies. This is 6 fewer than the amount of ladybugs. How many ladybugs are there?

Model it!

Answer:

Monday: 2 Arguments

Students have to reason about the information given to them and then decide which child they agree with and why.

Tuesday: Vocabulary Bingo

Students listen for the strategies and then cover 1 space at a time. Whoever gets 4 in a row, across, up or down or diagonally wins. The focus of this routine is on naming different addition and subtraction strategies.

Wednesday: Missing Numbers in a Two Hundred Grid

Students must use place value to fill in the empty spaces.

Thursday: Number Talk

Students discuss both addition and subtraction ways to make 15.

Friday: 3 Questions

Chorally read the problem 3 times before the students come up with questions.

Read the problem stem 3 times. The first time read it and ask about the context. The second time read it and talk about the numbers. The third time read it and ask what questions could be asked about the scenario. The teacher records these questions on the board. Then give the students time to think about the answers and discuss them.

Week 17 Activities

Monday: 2 Arguments

Look at the problem. Decide who you agree with. Discuss with your partner.

$$7 + \_\_\_ = 20$$

Jen said that the answer is 27. Kelly said the answer is 13. Who is correct? How do you know?

Tuesday: Vocabulary Bingo

Cover a take away from a number from itself fact. Cover a make 20 fact. Cover a take away ones from a teen fact. Cover a take away 10 fact. Cover a near neighbor fact (difference of 1 or 2).

As your teacher calls a type of fact, cover it and say the answer. For example, the teacher says, "a doubles fact." You have to cover a doubles fact and say the answer. ONLY cover 1 type of fact at a time.

1 + 2	10 − 4	8 − 2	7 + 5	12 + 2	20 − 4	17 − 1	16 + 4
9 + 1	6 + 6	5 + 6	2 − 2	16 − 10	9 + 5	5 + 5	8 + 4
6 + 14	4 + 3	12 − 2	17 − 10	5 − 3	9 + 8	12 − 2	6 + 6
15 + 1	18 + 2	15 − 5	7 + 7	13 + 2	8 − 7	8 − 8	9 − 7

Teacher call notes: Students have to cover the fact and then say the answer.
Cover a doubles fact. Cover a plus 1 fact. (Just the next number.) Cover a count on fact (plus 1, 2, or 3).
Cover a subtract from 10 fact. (Think ten friends.) Cover a take away or add zero fact.
Cover a count back fact (subtract 1, 2, or 3).
Cover a take away 1 fact. (Think the number before.) Cover a make ten fact.

Wednesday: Missing Numbers in a Two Hundred Grid

Fill in the missing numbers to the hundred grid puzzle.

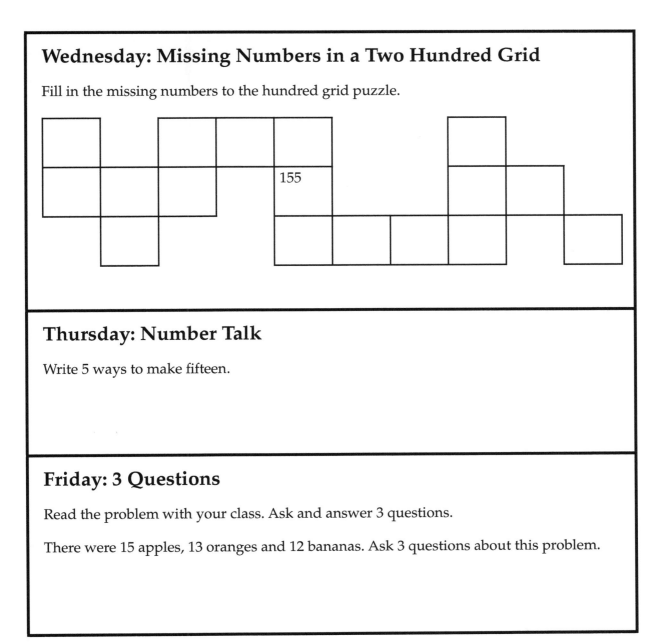

Thursday: Number Talk

Write 5 ways to make fifteen.

Friday: 3 Questions

Read the problem with your class. Ask and answer 3 questions.

There were 15 apples, 13 oranges and 12 bananas. Ask 3 questions about this problem.

Week 18 Teacher Notes

Monday: True or False?

In this routine the students discuss whether or not statements are true or false.

Tuesday: What Doesn't Belong?

In this routine students have to discuss what doesn't belong. They should be able to talk about what 3 of the boxes have in common and how the other one is different. There is often more than 1 thing that can be correct. The focus in this one is to name the types of facts that are alike and different.

Wednesday: Guess My Number

Students make up their own Guess my number by writing clues about their number. They can then share them out to the class or with a neighbor.

Thursday: Number Strings

Students discuss these expressions. The focus should be on how to add 10 to a number mentally.

Friday: Model That!

Students have to read, solve and model a word problem.

Monday: True or False?

Look at the boxes. Decide and discuss whether the equation is true or false.

True or false ?	True or false?	Make your own and share it out.
A. $12 + 2 = 6 + 6$	B. $11 - 1 = 9 + 1$	C.

Tuesday: What Doesn't Belong?

Look at the options in each box. Figure out which one doesn't belong. Decide and discuss.

A.

$20 + 40 + 10$	$20 + 20 + 40$
$100 - 30$	$10 + 10 + 50$

B.

$6 + 8$	$7 + 5$
$4 + 6$	$3 + 2$

Wednesday: Guess My Number

Use the clues to guess the number. Look at the hundred grid to help you figure out the number.

1	2	3	4	5	6	7	8	9	10
11	12	13	14	15	16	17	18	19	20
21	22	23	24	25	26	27	28	29	30
31	32	33	34	35	36	37	38	39	40
41	42	43	44	45	46	47	48	49	50
51	52	53	54	55	56	57	58	59	60
61	62	63	64	65	66	67	68	69	70
71	72	73	74	75	76	77	78	79	80
81	82	83	84	85	86	87	88	89	90
91	92	93	94	95	96	97	98	99	100

A. I am a 2-digit number. I am more than ____. I am less than ____. My digits add up to ____. Who am I?	B. The mystery number is 7. What are the clues?

Thursday: Number Strings

What are some ways to think about:

129 + 10
112 + 10
115 + 10
114 + 10

What do you notice about adding 10 to a number?

Friday: Model That!

Read and model the problem.

At the aquarium, in a pool we saw 8 turtles. This was 2 more than the fish that we saw. How many fish did we see? How many animals did we see altogether in the pool?

Model it in the twenty frame.

Week 19 Teacher Notes

Monday: Missing Numbers

Students have to reason about the missing numbers in the equation and solve them.

Tuesday: Vocabulary Bingo

Students listen for their strategies and then cover 1 space at a time. Whoever gets 4 in a row, across, up or down, or diagonally wins. The focus in this game is on discussing subtraction strategies.

Wednesday: Number Bond It!

This is an opportunity for students to build on their work on composing and decomposing numbers.

Thursday: Number Talk

Students work on subtracting numbers. They have to discuss whether or not they did it in their head, with a drawing or on paper.

Friday: What's the Story?

Students work on telling and solving word problems using a variety of models.

Week 19 Activities

Monday: Missing Numbers

Fill in the missing numbers.

___ + 2 = 5 + ___

12 + 7 = 9 + ___

____ + ____ = ____ + ____

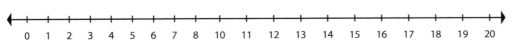

0 1 2 3 4 5 6 7 8 10 11 12 13 14 15 16 17 18 19 20

Tuesday: Vocabulary Bingo

As your teacher calls a strategy, cover one fact that matches that strategy. Cover only 1 space at a time.

Teacher will call out:
Taking away 1 (it's the number before).
Take away a number from itself (always zero).
Take away a number from 10 (think 10 friends).
Take away neighbor numbers (difference of 1 or 2).
Taking away 0 from a number (number stays the same).
Count back facts (count back 1, 2, or 3).
Take away ten from a teen.
Take away ones from a teen.
Half Facts.
Bridge Ten (use ten as a bridge to subtract).
Partial differences (take away part of the number at a time).

14 − 1	20 − 10	14 − 4	19 − 18
9 − 9	17 − 7	20 − 10	10 − 2
14 − 7	10 − 4	8 − 5	15 − 7
20 − 2	17 − 9	5 − 3	10 − 8

8 − 8	7 − 5	5 − 1	10 − 3
20 − 10	5 − 3	18 − 9	17 − 16
10 − 0	13 − 10	10 − 4	12 − 10
11 − 8	12 − 6	11 − 9	16 − 8

Wednesday: Number Bond It!

Show how to break apart 25 in 3 different ways!

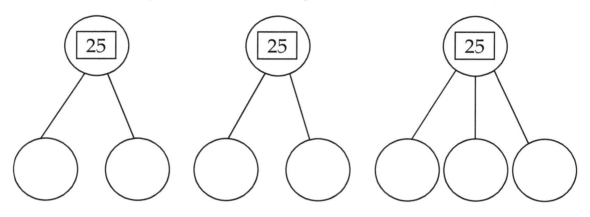

Thursday: Number Talk

Pick a number from each circle. Make a subtraction problem. Write the problem under the way you solved it. For example, I did 62 – 18 on an open number line.

Did I do it in my head?	Did I use a model?	Did I write down the numbers and solve it on paper?

A.

21   62
34   47
53   65
78   81   90
100

B.

18   10   9   5

20   13   4
2   16
8   9   5   7

Friday: What's the Story?

Write a word problem where the answer is 30 oranges.

Story

Model

Equation

Week 20 Teacher Notes

Monday: True or False?

In this routine the students discuss whether or not statements are true or false.

Tuesday: Vocabulary Tic Tac Toe

Students play rock, paper, scissors to see who starts the game. They then take turns picking a square and describing the shape and then putting an x or an o. Whoever gets 3 in a row first wins.

At the end of the game, go over the possible answers with the entire class. Have students discuss what they wrote as answers.

Wednesday: What Doesn't Belong?

In this routine students have to discuss what doesn't belong. They should be able to talk about what 3 of the boxes have in common and how the other one is different. There is often more than 1 thing that can be correct.

Thursday: Number Strings

Students are looking at patterns in expressions. They should notice that these are numbers where you can use the bridge ten strategy.

Friday: Problem Solving

Students work on solving word problems with a variety of models. They should recognize that this is a compare problem.

Monday: True or False?

Look at the boxes. Decide and discuss whether the equation is true or false.

	True or False?
$8 + 10 = 4 + 5 + 5 + 4$	
$12 - 6 = 20 - 14$	
$20 = 15 - 5$	
$5 - 5 = 10 - 5$	
Make your own!	

Tuesday: Vocabulary Tic Tac Toe

Play rock, paper, scissors to see who starts the game. Then take turns picking a square and describing the shape and then putting an x or an o. Whoever gets 3 in a row first wins.

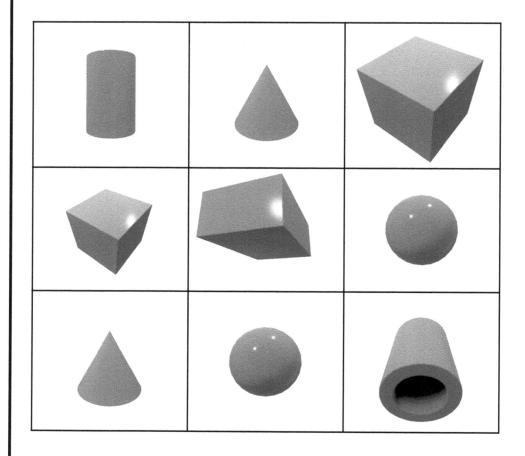

Wednesday: What Doesn't Belong?

Look at the options in each box. Figure out which one doesn't belong. Decide and Discuss.

cone	rectangular prism
sphere	cylinder

12 – 2	100 – 90
80 – 10	4 + 6

Thursday: Number Strings

What are some ways to think about these problems:

15 – 7
16 – 9
17 – 8

What do you notice?

Friday: Problem Solving

In the aquarium there were 10 animals. 5 were turtles. The rest were fish. Then, 5 more fish came. How many fish are there now? How many animals are there now?

Draw it!

Week 21 Teacher Notes

Monday: What Doesn't Belong?

Students have to figure out which one doesn't belong in the group.

Tuesday: Vocabulary Tic Tac Toe

Play with a partner. Play rock, paper, scissors to see who starts first. Take turns picking a square and discussing the word. Draw a picture or write about the word. Then, put an x or an o in the box. Whoever gets 3 in a row first wins.

At the end of the game, go over the possible answers with the entire class. Have students discuss what they wrote as answers.

Wednesday: Convince Me!

Students have to prove that the equation is true.

Thursday: Number Strings

Students discuss different ways to solve the problems.

Friday: Model That!

Students have to read, model and solve the problem.

Monday: What Doesn't Belong?

Look at the boxes and decide which one doesn't belong in each set.

A.

100 – 40	90 – 50
60 – 20	70 – 30

B.

35 + 35	20 + 20 + 20 + 10
50 + 20	20 + 60

Tuesday: Vocabulary Tic Tac Toe

Play with a partner. Play rock, paper, scissors to see who starts first. Take turns picking a square and discussing the word. Draw a picture or write about the word. Then, put an x or an o in the box. Whoever gets 3 in a row first wins.

sum	ones	square
odd	bar graph	count on
make ten/ ten friends	doubles	equation

difference	tens	hexagon
even	addend	picture graph
doubles plus 1 or near doubles	digit	fewer

Wednesday: Convince Me!

Prove it with numbers, words and/or pictures!

$80 - 25 = 55$

1	2	3	4	5	6	7	8	9	10
11	12	13	14	15	16	17	18	19	20
21	22	23	24	25	26	27	28	29	30
31	32	33	34	35	36	37	38	39	40
41	42	43	44	45	46	47	48	49	50
51	52	53	54	55	56	57	58	59	60
61	62	63	64	65	66	67	68	69	70
71	72	73	74	75	76	77	78	79	80
81	82	83	84	85	86	87	88	89	90
91	92	93	94	95	96	97	98	99	100

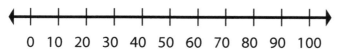

0 10 20 30 40 50 60 70 80 90 100

Thursday: Number Strings

What are some ways to think about and show:

$$81 - 19$$
$$74 - 17$$
$$52 - 18$$

What do you notice?

Friday: Model That!

Read and model the problem.

Mom gave Katy 5 stickers. Katy gave her sister 2 of them. Dad gave Katie 4 more stickers. How many stickers does Katie have now?

Draw it!

Answer:

Week 22 Teacher Notes

Monday: Magic Squares

Add up all the numbers to find the magic number. It will be the same sum in all directions.

Tuesday: Vocabulary Tic Tac Toe

Students play with a partner. They do rock, paper, scissors to see who starts first. They take turns picking a square and discussing the word. They have to draw a picture or write about the word. Then, put an x or an o in the box. Whoever gets 3 in a row first wins.

At the end of the game, go over the possible answers with the entire class. Have students discuss what they wrote as answers.

Wednesday: Number Line It!

Students have to discuss how to order and plot the numbers on the number line from least to greatest

Thursday: Number Talk

Students review adding one and 2-digit numbers.

Friday: Sort That!

Students have to read and reason about word problems. They have to sort out the different types of problems.

Week 22 Activities

Monday: Magic Squares

Add up all the numbers to find the magic number. It will be the same sum in all directions.

A.

8		
	5	
6		2

B.

6		
7		3

Tuesday: Vocabulary Tic Tac Toe

Play with a partner. Play rock, paper, scissors to see who starts first. Take turns picking a square and discussing the word. Draw a picture or write about the word. Then, put an x or an o in the box. Whoever gets 3 in a row first wins.

Explain to your partner how you would solve this problem. Can you name your strategy?

Game 1

9 - 9	7 - 1	8 - 0
14 - 7	10 - 2	14 - 10
12 - 2	6 - 2	8 - 7

Game 2

3 + 3	3 + 4	3 + 5
4 + 1	4 + 2	4 + 3
5 + 5	10 + 5	4 + 0

Wednesday: Number Line It!

Place these numbers on the number line. Try to be as exact as possible.

67 42 19 99 51 83

0   100

Compare these with your partner. Explain your thinking. How do you know you are correct?

Thursday: Number Talk

Pick a number from each circle Add them. Then, explain how you did it. Write the problem under the way you solved it. For example, 28 + 12. I can do that in my head because it is a ten friend.

Did I do it in my head?	Did I use a model?	Did I write down the numbers and solve it on paper?

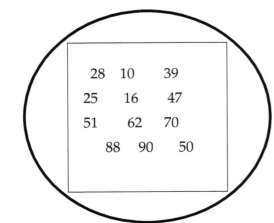

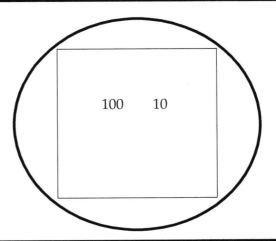

Friday: Sort That!

Put a line under the take away problems. Put a circle around the join problems. Answer all the problems.

Justify your thinking with a partner and then share with a whole group.

1. Sue had 5 marbles. She got 15 more. How many does she have now?

2. Luke had 50 marbles. He gave 15 away. How many does he have now?

3. Marco had 77 marbles. His brother gave him 12 more. How many does he have now?

4. Maria had 88 marbles. She got some more. Now she has 99. How many did she get?

Week 23 Teacher Notes

Monday: Always, Sometimes, Never

Students have to discuss whether or not the statement is always, sometimes or never true.

Tuesday: Vocabulary Bingo

Students populate the Bingo board with the words. The teacher calls out the words by defining them or showing a picture or some sort of example. Students cross out the words on their boards. Whoever gets 4 in a row or all 4 corners first wins.

Be sure that the students put the words all over the board.

Wednesday: Number of the Day

Students have to fill in the boxes to represent the number 78. Have the students do it on their own, discuss with a partner and then debrief with the whole class.

Thursday: Number Strings

The focus of this conversation is on bridging 10 anytime there is a 7, 8 or 9.

Friday: Model That!

In this activity students are working on modeling problems in different ways.

Week 23 Activities

Monday: Always, Sometimes, Never

Read the statement and decide if it is always, sometimes or never true.

If you add 2 numbers the answer will always be even.

Tuesday: Vocabulary Bingo

Words: decompose, compose, equation, expression, halves, fourths, hundred, hexagon, quarter, rectangle, strategy, square

Write a word in each space. Your teacher will call out the description of the word or show you a picture and you cross out the word. Whoever gets 4 in a row or all 4 corners win.

Wednesday: Number of the Day

Fill in the boxes based on the number 78.

78

Number in word form	Show 1 addition sentence that makes 78.
Show 1 subtraction sentence that makes 78.	Add 3 numbers that make 78.

Thursday: Number Strings

What are some ways to think about and show:

String 1	String 2
19 + 7	18 + 5
19 + 6	28 + 5
19 + 5	38 + 6
19 + 4	48 + 7
	58 + 8

Friday: Model That!

Read and model the problem.

Sue jumped 15″, 27″ and then 19″. How far did she jump in total?

Model on the open number line.

⬅————————————————————————➡

A.

1	2	3	4	5	6	7	8	9	10
11	12	13	14	15	16	17	18	19	20
21	22	23	24	25	26	27	28	29	30
31	32	33	34	35	36	37	38	39	40
41	42	43	44	45	46	47	48	49	50
51	52	53	54	55	56	57	58	59	60
61	62	63	64	65	66	67	68	69	70
71	72	73	74	75	76	77	78	79	80
81	82	83	84	85	86	87	88	89	90
91	92	93	94	95	96	97	98	99	100

B. Model using the break apart strategy. (Add the tens and then the ones.)

Monday: Magic Square

Students have to put in numbers so that they add up to 15 in any direction.

Tuesday: It Is/It Isn't

Students have to discuss the number 73 using the framework it is/it isn't. The word bank should scaffold the discussion.

Wednesday: Greater Than, Less Than, in Between

This is a place value routine where students have to discuss numbers within the framework of greater than, less than and in between.

Thursday: Number Talk

Students discuss strategies for solving the problem.

Friday: Picture That!

Students make up a word problem about the picture.

Monday: Magic Square

Fill in the blanks so that all that they add up to 15 in all directions.

8		6
	5	

Tuesday: It Is/It Isn't

Decide and discuss what the number is and is not.

73

It Is	It Isn't

Word bank: 2-digit, 1-digit, less than, greater than, in between, 10 more than, 10 less than, more than, before, after.

Wednesday: Greater Than, Less Than, in Between

Fill in the boxes based on the numbers.

50   125   390

Name a number less than 50	Name a number less than 125	Name a number greater than 125
Name a number greater than 390	Name a number in between 50 and125	Name a number in between 125 and 390

Thursday: Number Talk

What are some ways to subtract 54 – 19?

Friday: Picture That!

Tell a story about this box of donuts. Write an equation that can be used to represent the story you created.

Story:

Equation:

Monday: 2 Arguments

Students have to reason about the given situation, decide who they agree with and defend their thinking.

Tuesday: Vocabulary Draw

Students have to draw something to represent each word.

Wednesday: Money Problems

Students are given a number and have to show several ways to represent the number.

Thursday: Number Talk

Students work on adding 2 2-digit numbers and describing their strategies.

Friday: Make Your Own Problem

Students make their own problem by filling in numbers. They have to then model it and write a number sentence and share their thinking with their math partner.

Week 25 Activities

Monday: 2 Arguments

Look at the problem. Decide who you agree with. Discuss with your partner.

$$12 + \rule{1cm}{0.4pt} = 50$$

Maya said the answer was 38.

Maria said the answer was 62.

Who do you agree with?

Why?

Tuesday: Vocabulary Draw

Read the word. Draw an example. Explain what it is.

Word	Draw it	Explain it
even number		
hexagon		
equation		
expanded form		
odd number		

Wednesday: Money Problems

Raul had 25 cents. Show 3 different combinations of coins he could have had.

Way 1	Way 2	Way 3

Thursday: Number Talk

Pick a number from each circle. Add them. Then, explain how you did it. Write the problem under the way you solved it. For example, 8 + 2. I can do that in my head because it is a ten friend.

Did I do it in my head?	Did I use a model?	Did I write down the numbers and solve it on paper?

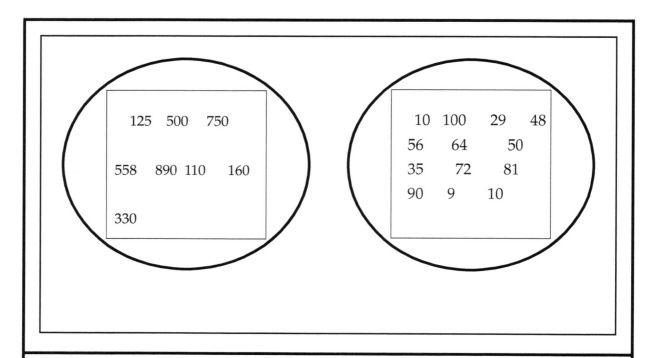

Friday: Make Your Own Problem

Fill in the blanks.

Use 2-digit numbers.

Lucy had _____ marbles. She got _____ more for her birthday. How many does she have now?

Model it!

Number sentence (equation):

Week 26 Teacher Notes

Monday: It Is/It Isn't

Students have to discuss the word using this frame.

Tuesday: Vocabulary 1-Minute Essay

Students have to discuss and write about the word.

Wednesday: Find and Fix the Error

Students have to reason about a problem and decide what is the error and fix it.

Thursday: Number Strings

Students are looking at patterns in expressions.

The focus in this conversation is bridging 10 when there is a 7, 8 or 9.

Friday: Equation Match

Students have to match the equation with the story.

Week 26 Activities

Monday: It Is/It Isn't

Decide and discuss what the shape is and is not.

Rectangle

It Is	It Isn't

Word bank: shape, polygon, straight sides, closed sides, curved sides, open sides, straight lines, 2D, 3D, quadrilateral, angles, vertices.

Tuesday: Vocabulary 1-Minute Essay

(For 30 seconds) Write everything you can about polygons. Use numbers, words and pictures.

(15 seconds) Now switch with a neighbor and add 1 thing to their list.

(15 seconds) Now add 1 more thing to your list.

Wednesday: Find and Fix the Error

Read the problem. Find and fix the mistake.

John did this. The answer is wrong. Find and fix the error.

$$\begin{array}{r} 100 \\ -\ 29 \\ \hline 129 \end{array}$$

1. What is the mistake?
2. Why can't you do what John did?
3. Fix it.
4. Explain your thinking to your partner and then the whole group.

Thursday: Number Strings

What are some ways to think about and show:

$$28 + 4$$
$$19 + 24$$
$$27 + 24$$
$$58 + 37$$

Friday: Equation Match

Match the story with the correct equation.

Jan had some marbles. She got 20 more. Now she has 100. How many did she have in the beginning?

A. $20 + \bigcirc = \bigcirc$

B. $\bigcirc + 20 = 100$

C. $100 + 20 = \bigcirc$

D. Equation is not here.

Week 27 Teacher Notes

Monday: 3 Truths and a Fib

Students have to read the statements and figure out which one is not true.

Tuesday: Vocabulary Brainstorm

Students have to describe the word.

Wednesday: Complete the Pattern

Students have to discuss and then complete the patterns.

Thursday: Number Talk

Students discuss subtracting a number from 100. Be sure to use models and talk about counting up, partial differences and counting back on an open number line.

Friday: Equation Match

Students have match the equation to the problem it represents.

Week 27 Activities

Monday: 3 Truths and a Fib

Which one is false? Why? Explain to your neighbor and then the group.

50 is greater than 100	70 is not less than 10
5 tens is the same as 50 ones	100 is less than 120

Tuesday: Vocabulary Brainstorm

In each thought cloud write or draw something that has to do with measurement.

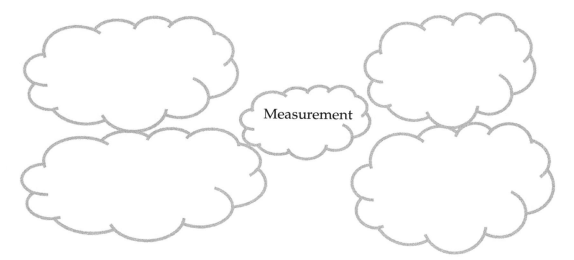

Measurement

Wednesday: Complete the Pattern

Complete and describe the pattern.

1. 110, 210, _____, _____, _____, 610,___

2. 55, ___, 75, ____, 95, ___, 115, ____, ____

3. Make your own:

____, ____,____, ____,____, ____,____, ____,

Thursday: Number Talk

What are some ways to solve 100 – 68?

Friday: Equation Match

Look at the set-up equation. Match it to the problem it represents.

$$1{,}000 - \bigcirc = 900$$

Problem A	Problem B
The store had 1,000 marbles. They got 900 more. How many do they have now?	The store had 1,000 marbles. They sold some. Now they have 900. How many did they sell?

Monday: True or False?

Students have to reason about whether or not the problem is true or false.

Tuesday: Vocabulary Tic Tac Toe

Students play with a partner. They do rock, paper, scissors to see who starts first. They take turns picking a square and discussing the word. They have to draw a picture or write about the word. Then, put an x or an o in the box. Whoever gets 3 in a row first wins.

At the end of the game, go over the possible answers with the entire class. Have students discuss what they wrote as answers.

Wednesday: Missing Numbers

Students have to reason about what the missing numbers are.

Thursday: Number Talk

Students should discuss different ways to subtract.

Friday: Model That!

Students have to discuss and model the problem

Week 28 Activities

Monday: True or False?

Decide if the equation is true or false.

$$2 + 7 = 19 - 10$$

1. Think about it.
2. Share your thinking with a friend. Defend your answer.
3. Share your thinking with the group.
4. Write another equation that is similar.

Tuesday: Vocabulary Tic Tac Toe

Play rock, paper, scissors to see who starts the game. Take turns picking squares. Before you mark it with an x or o you have to write the definition or draw a picture of the item in the square. Whoever gets 3 in a row first, wins.

numeral	addend	word form
equal	fraction	digit
equation	estimate	expanded form

fourths	greater	quarter
ruler	alike	compare
sphere	one half	cylinder

Wednesday: Missing Numbers

What are the missing numbers in the problems below?

A.

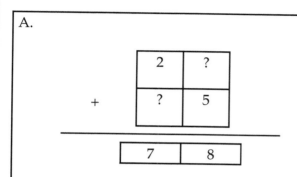

B.

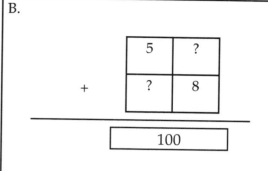

Thursday: Number Talk

Pick a number from each circle. Make a subtraction problem. Write the problem under the way you solved it. For example, 18 - 9. I can do that in my head because it is half fact.

Did I do it in my head?	Did I use a model?	Did I write down the numbers and solve it on paper?

A.

28   11
84 55 70
43 36 99
62 100

B.

8 9 7 5
14 19 10
  12 33 40
50 25 62
70 80 90
9 10

Friday: Model That!

Read, model and solve the problem.

Hong had 25 marbles. He had 20 more than Joe. How many did Joe have? How many did they have altogether?

Solve with a tape/strip diagram.

Week 29 Teacher Notes

Monday: Convince Me!

Students have to reason about and then prove that the statement is true with words, numbers or models.

Tuesday: Vocabulary Talk

Students should discuss with your partner and then the class what these words mean. Give examples.

Wednesday: Skip Counting

Students discuss patterns in skip counting by different numbers.

Thursday: Number Strings

Students work on subtracting 10 and 100 from numbers.

Friday: What's the Story?

Students have to write a story that matches the model.

Week 29 Activities

Monday: Convince Me!

Convince me that:
$14 + 6 + 12 = 20 + 12$

Tuesday: Vocabulary Talk

Discuss with your partner and then the class what these words mean. Give examples.

Justify

Defend

Convince me

Wednesday: Skip Counting

Name 2 numbers between 100 and 120 that you would say if you were skip counting by 2s.

Name 2 numbers greater than 500 that you would say if you were skip counting by 5s.

Name 2 numbers greater than 100 that you would say if you were skip counting by 10s starting with number 27.

Thursday: Number Strings

What are some ways to think about and show:

$$505 - 10$$
$$400 - 10$$
$$679 - 100$$
$$908 - 100$$

Friday: What's the Story?

Write a word problem about this array.

Story:

Equation:

Week 30 Teacher Notes

Monday: Magic Square

Students have to fill in numbers so that the sum makes 15 in all directions.

Tuesday: Vocabulary Tic Tac Toe

Students play with a partner. They do rock, paper, scissors to see who starts first. They take turns picking a square and discussing the word. They have to draw a picture or write about the word. Then, put an x or an o in the box. Whoever gets 3 in a row first wins.

At the end of the game, go over the possible answers with the entire class. Have students discuss what they wrote as answers.

Wednesday: Number of the Day

Students have to represent the number in a variety of ways.

Thursday: Number Talk

Students have to discuss solving the problem.

The focus should be on different strategies that could be used to get to the answer. What are different ways they could work with numbers to get the answer?

Friday: Tell a Word Problem About This Equation

Students have to tell a word problem about the equation.

Monday: Magic Square

Fill in the squares so that the numbers in any direction adds to 15. Check going up, down, and sideways.

6		8
	5	

Tuesday: Vocabulary Tic Tac Toe

Play rock, paper, scissors to see who starts the game. Take turns picking squares. Before you mark it with an x or o you have to write the definition or draw a picture of the item in the square. Whoever gets 3 in a row first, wins.

Use in an example. Write it down.

<	+	greater than
>	–	equal to
more than	=	less than

Draw the picture.

trapezoid	pentagon	rectangular prism
sphere	square	cylinder
cone	rectangle	hexagon

Wednesday: Number of the Day

Fill in the boxes based on the number.

507

Word Form	10 more	10 less
expanded form	_____ + _____ = 507	_____ − _____ = 507
Base ten sketch	How many more to 1,000	odd or even
100 more	100 less	507 − _____ = _____

Thursday: Number Talk

What are the missing numbers in the problems below?

A. 72 + ? = 133	B. 498 + ? = 1000

Friday: Tell a Word Problem About This Equation

$$60 + 40 = 100$$

Story

Model

Equation

Week 31 Teacher Notes

Monday: Venn Diagram

Students have to read the criteria in the rectangles and then fill in the Venn diagram accordingly.

Tuesday: Vocabulary Bingo

Students populate the board and then lay Bingo. The teacher calls the words by showing example and giving definitions. Whoever crosses out 4 in a row first wins.

Be sure that students write the words in different parts of their boards.

Wednesday: Why Is It Not?

In this routine, students have to discuss why a particular answer is incorrect.

Thursday: Number Talk

Students are working on different ways to model addition problems and discuss their work.

Friday: What's the Question?

Students will read the problem 3 times and focus on the story, then the numbers and then possible questions. They should brainstorm them and then answer them.

Monday: Venn Diagram

Look at the rectangles. Fill in the Venn diagram.

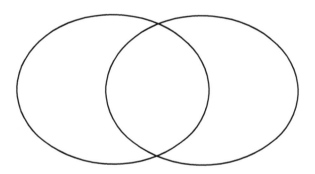

Numbers less than 200

Numbers greater than 500

Numbers that have a 7 in the tens place

Tuesday: Vocabulary Bingo

Write a word in each space. Be sure to write your words all over the board.

Words: array, fraction, picture graph, addend, bar graph, centimeter, column, row, equal group, fourths, halves, thirds.

Wednesday: Why Is It Not?

Write a word in each space. Be sure to write your words all over the board. Your teacher will call out the description of the word or show you a picture and you cross out the word. Whoever gets 4 in a row or all 4 corners win.

Think about it. Talk about it with a partner. Share with the class.

A. 12 = _____ + 6 Why is it not 18?	B. 10 = _____ − 2 Why is it not 8?

Thursday: Number Talk

Pick a number from each circle. Make an addition problem. Write the problem under the way you solved it. For example, 28 + 19. I can do that in my head by making the problem 27 + 20. I can do that in my head by making the problem 27 + 20.

Did I do it in my head?	Did I use a model?	Did I write down the numbers and solve it on paper?

A.

```
18    44
16    37
24    59    63
99    80    77
```

B.

```
8    9    5
6    4    7
11   22   40   37
50   13   54   65
79   81   90
```

Friday: What's the Question?

Read together out loud with your class 3 times.

1st time: Think about what the story is about.
2nd time: Think about what the numbers mean.
3rd time: Come up with some questions about the story and answer them.

The bakery had 25 lemon cookies, 15 sugar cookies and 10 chocolate chip cookies.	What are some questions that you can ask?

Week 32 Teacher Notes

Monday: Magic Square

Students have to fill in the square so that the sum is 15 in all directions.

Tuesday: Vocabulary Brainstorm

Students have to write about the word using numbers, words and pictures in the clouds.

Wednesday: 3 Truths and a Fib

Students have to discuss the statements and decide which one is false.

Thursday: Number Talk

Students discuss subtracting from 100. Discussion should include using various strategies, such as partial differences, compensation (adding 2 to each number to get an easier problem) and counting up.

Friday: Word Problem Sort

Students have to reason about and sort the different word problems.

Monday: Magic Square

Sum is 15. Fill in the empty squares in all directions so that it makes 15.

2		6
	5	

Tuesday: Vocabulary Brainstorm

In each thought cloud write or draw something that has to do with fractions.

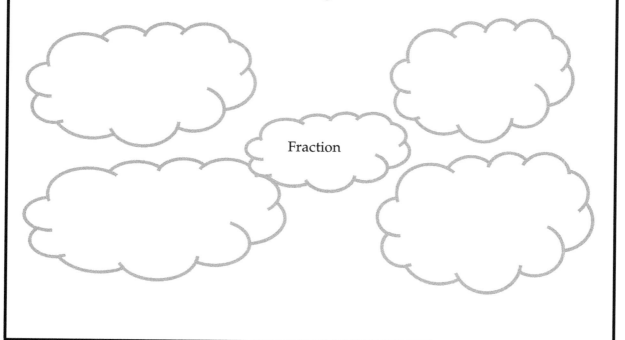

Fraction

Wednesday: 3 Truths and a Fib

Look at the four boxes and decide which one has something that is not true.

100 − 90 = 10	9 tens minus 8 tens is 1 ten
20 + 20 + 40 + 10 = 90	900 + 10 = 1,000

Thursday: Number Talk

What are some ways to subtract 1,000 − 418?

Friday: Word Problem Sort

Circle the compare problem. How do you know it is a compare problem? Are you looking for the bigger part, the smaller part or the difference? Solve it.

A. Larry has 15 car stickers and 27 truck stickers. How many stickers does he have altogether?

B. Marta has 35 rings. She has 20 more than her sister. How many does her sister have?

C. Hong had 20 toy cars. His sister gave him 10 more. How many does he have now?

Monday: What Doesn't Belong?

Students have to decide which clocks don't belong and they have to explain why and tell the time on the other clocks.

Tuesday: Frayer Model

Students have to discuss the word fraction using the frayer model as a frame.

Wednesday: Number of the Day

Students have to fill in the boxes to represent the number 443. Have the students do it on their own, discuss with a partner and then debrief whole class.

Thursday: Number Talk

Students have to discuss this subtraction problem and different ways to solve it.

Friday: What's the Question?

Students have to read the scenario and come up with 3 possible questions.

Monday: What Doesn't Belong?

Find the one that does not belong in each set.

A.

B.

Tuesday: Frayer Model

Fill in the boxes based on the word.

Fraction

Definition	Examples
Give a picture example	Non-examples

Wednesday: Number of the Day

Fill in the boxes based on the number.

443

Word form	10 more	10 less
Expanded form	_____ + _____ = 443	_____ – _____ = 443
Base ten sketch	How many more to 1,000	Odd or even?
100 more	100 less	443 – _____ = _____

Thursday: Number Talk

What are some ways to think about and show:

$$85 - 59$$

Friday: What's the Question?

Read together out loud with your class 3 times.

1st time: Think about what the story is about.
2nd time: think about what the numbers mean.
3rd time: Come up with some questions about the story and answer them.

Think of at least 2 questions you could ask about this story. Write them down. Discuss with your classmates.

Lucy has 25 red marbles, 17 blue ones and 39 green ones.

1)
2)

Week 34 Teacher Notes

Monday: Convince Me!

Students have to read and reason about a statement and decide and defend why it is true.

Tuesday: Frayer Model

Students discuss and write about the word using the frayer model as a frame.

Wednesday: Guess My Number

Students use the clues to guess the number.

Thursday: Number Talk

Students discuss subtraction strategies for this problem.

Friday: Picture That!

Students use the picture prompt to tell and represent a story.

Monday: Convince Me!

Read the problems and convince me that they are true.

A.	B.
If you add an even number and an odd number you get an odd number.	If you add an odd number and an odd number you get an even number.
Prove it with numbers, words and pictures:	Prove it with numbers, words and pictures:

Tuesday: Frayer Model

Fill in the boxes based on the word.

Length

Definition	Examples
Give a picture example	Non-examples

Wednesday: Guess My Number

Read the clues and guess the number.

A. I am a 2-digit number. I am greater than 19 and less than 30. I am odd. The sum of my digits is greater than 8 and less than 11. Who am I?	B. I am a 2-digit number. I am less than 100. I am greater than 80. I am less than 90 − 4. I am an even number. The difference between my digits is 6. Who am I?

Thursday: Number Talk

What are some ways to think about and show:

$$188 + 249?$$

Friday: Picture That!

Write an array problem about the picture.

1. Story

2. Model

3. Equation

Week 35 Teacher Notes

Monday: Tic Tac Toe

Students play rock, paper, scissors to see who starts. They take turns telling time in the squares. They put an x or an o to mark their square. Whoever gets 3 in a row first wins.

Tuesday: Vocabulary Fill-in

Students fill in the missing vocabulary words.

Wednesday: Missing Numbers

Students have to reaon about which numbers are missing in the problem.

Thursday: Number Talk

Students discuss strategies for adding 3-digit numbers.

Friday: What's the Question?

In this routine, students have to read the problem 3 times and then ask and answer questions about the problem.

Week 35 Activities

Monday: Tic Tac Toe

Play rock, paper, scissors to determine who goes first. Take turns telling time in the squares. Put an x or an o to mark the square that you did. Whoever gets 3 in a row first, wins.

A.

B.

Tuesday: Vocabulary Fill-in

Fill in the sentences with the correct word.

Word bank: even, difference, array, sum.

a. The answer to an addition problem is called the _____.

b. Things lined up in columns and rows can be called an _____.

c. The answer to a subtraction problem is called the _____.

d. A number that can be split up equally is called an _____ number.

Wednesday: Missing Numbers

What are the missing numbers in the problems below?

A.

	?	8	?
+	2	?	4

7 9 0

B.

_____ + 719 = 901

Thursday: Number Talk

What are some ways to think about and show:

$$278 + 199$$

Friday: What's the Question?

Read 3 times out loud with class.

1st time: Think about what the story is about.
2nd time: Think about what the numbers mean.
3rd time: Come up with some questions about the story and answer them.

Think of at least 2 questions you could ask about this story. Write them down. Discuss with your classmates.

The store has 12 footballs, 20 soccer balls and 18 baseballs.

1)
2)

Monday: What Doesn't Belong?

Students have to figure out what doesn't belong.

Tuesday: Vocabulary 1-Minute Essay

Students write about the word array.

Wednesday: Fraction of the Day

Students represent fractions using the template.

Thursday: Number Talk

Students work on subtracting numbers and thinking about the differences between them.

Friday: Make Your Own Story

Students are given the answer and they have to make up their own story.

Monday: What Doesn't Belong?

Find the one that does not belong in each set.

A.

2 + 38	19 + 19
40 − 2	28 + 10

B.

350 − 100	260 − 10
1,000 − 250	450 − 200

Tuesday: Vocabulary 1-Minute Essay

(For 30 seconds) Write everything you can about array. Use numbers words and pictures.

(15 seconds) Now switch with a neighbor and add 1 thing to their list.

(15 seconds) Now add 1 more thing to your list.

Wednesday: Fraction of the Day

Fill in the boxes based on the fraction.

$$\frac{1}{4}$$

Word form	Rectangle model
Circle model	Non-example

Thursday: Number Talk

A. Subtract 2 numbers that have a difference of about 100.

B. Subtract 2 numbers that have a difference of about 250.

Friday: Make Your Own Story.

Write a word problem where the answer is 17 marbles.

Story:

Equation:

Model:

Solution:

Week 37 Teacher Notes

Monday: Number Bond It!

Students have to decompose a number in a variety of ways.

Tuesday: Vocabulary 1-Minute Essay

Students should write about some things they have learned in math this year. Then, they should share that with a partner and then with the whole class.

Wednesday: Fraction of the Day

Students look at the fraction and then fill in the squares based on that fraction.

Thursday: Number Talk

Students work on adding numbers and thinking about the differences between them.

Friday: What's the Story?

In this routine, the students are given a tape diagram and asked to tell a story about the numbers that are modeled on it.

Week 37 Activities

Monday: Number Bond It!

Show how to decompose 500 in 3 different ways!

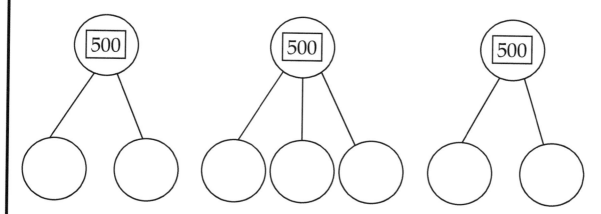

Tuesday: Vocabulary 1-Minute Essay

Write some important things that you have learned about math this year.

Then turn and discuss what you written with a partner. Be ready to discuss with the whole group.

Wednesday: Fraction of the Day

Look at the fraction. Fill in the squares based on the fraction.

$$\frac{1}{2}$$

Word form	Rectangle model
Circle model	Non-example

Thursday: Number Talk

Pick a number from each circle. Add them. Decide how you will solve it and write that expression under the title.

Did I do it in my head?	Did I use a model?	Did I write down the numbers and solve it on paper?

A.

12   23
34   46   57
68   79   84
100

B.

Put your own numbers:

Friday: What's the Story?

Look at the model. Write a story that matches the model.

15

15	3

Story

Equation

Week 38 Teacher Notes

Monday: Graphs

Students have to read the frequency table, make a bar graph and then ask and answer 3 questions about the data.

Tuesday: Vocabulary Tic Tac Toe

Students have to discuss the words with their partner. They have to draw or write or explain their thinking before they put the x or o. Whoever gets 3 in a row first wins.

Answers vary.

At the end of the game, go over the possible answers with the entire class. Have students discuss what they wrote as answers.

Wednesday: Missing Numbers

Students have to fill in the blanks to make the statement true.

Thursday: Number Talk

In this number talk, students will make up their own problems. They will write 5 numbers into each circle and decide whether they want to add or subtract. They will then solve their problem and discuss how they did it.

Friday: Problem Solving

Solve and model the problem.

Monday: Graphs

Use the information below to do the activities.

Our Favorite Animals

Animals	Votes
dogs	16
cats	10
birds	4
fish	12
other	2

Make a Bar Graph with the data.
Make a scale by skip counting by 2s.
Label the title, the categories and the scale.

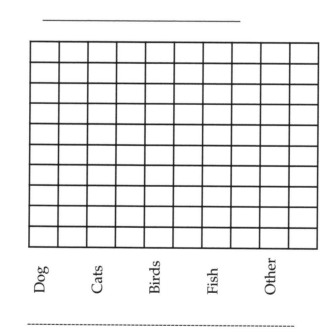

Ask 3 questions about this graph.

Tuesday: Vocabulary Tic Tac Toe

Play this game with your math partner. For each word that you pick, draw a picture or write a definition on the side. Then, put an x or an o. Whoever gets 3 in a row first wins.

frequency table	picture graph	bar graph
tally chart	categories	data
difference	sum	title

make ten	bridge ten	count back
count on	difference of 1	doubles plus 2
half fact	doubles plus 1	doubles

Wednesday: Missing Numbers

Fill in the blanks to make the statement true.

_____ + _____ > _____ + _____ + _____

Thursday: Number Talk

Pick a number from each circle Add them. Then, decide how you are going to solve it. Write the problem under the way you solved it.

Did I do it in my head?	Did I use a model?	Did I write down the numbers and solve it on paper?

Write in 5 2-digit numbers.   Write in 5 2-digit numbers.

Friday: Problem Solving

Read, model and solve the problem.

There were 10 animals. 5 were turtles. The rest were fish. Then some more fish came. Now there are 7 fish. How many fish came? How many animals are there altogether?

Model:

Answer:

Week 39 Teacher Notes

Monday: Graphs

Students have to read the information in the chart. Use it to make a graph and then ask questions about the graph.

Tuesday: Vocabulary Tic Tac Toe

Students have to discuss with their partner the types of strategies they would use to solve the problems. Whoever gets 3 in a row first wins.

Answers vary.

At the end of the game, go over the possible answers with the entire class. Have students discuss what they wrote as answers.

Wednesday: Number Bond It!

Students have to break apart the numbers in different ways.

Thursday: Number Talk

Students have to write in 4 numbers in each circle. Pick a number from each circle. Make a subtraction problem. Then, solve it. They must write the problem under the way they solved it.

Friday: Make Your Own Story

Students have to make up their own story and model and solve it.

Monday: Graphs

Use the information below to do the activities.

Our Favorite Animals

Animals	Votes
dogs	10
cats	6
other	2

Make a picture graph with the data.

_____

dogs	
cats	
other	

Key

 = 2 votes

Ask 3 questions about this graph.

Tuesday: Vocabulary Tic Tac Toe

Play rock, paper, scissors to see who starts the game. Take turns picking squares. Before you mark it with an x or o you have to name the strategy you are using to solve the problem. Whoever gets 3 in a row first, wins.

10 − 0	5 − 4	10 − 8
18 − 10	15 − 5	14 − 12
12 − 6	8 − 6	20 − 8

Strategy bank: subtracting zero, subtracting a number from itself, using ten friends, counting back, difference of 1 or 2, take away ten, take away ones from a teen, difference of 2, half facts, bridge ten, count up, use ten as a landmark.

Wednesday: Number Bond It!

Show how to decompose 1,000 in 3 different ways!

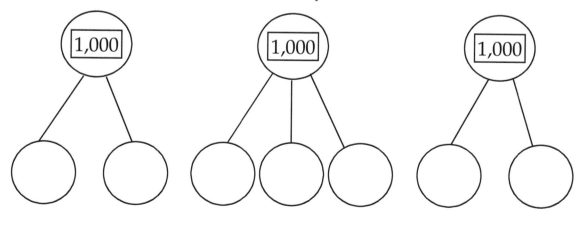

Thursday: Number Talk

Pick a number from each circle. Make a subtraction problem. Write the problem under the way you solved it.

Did I do it in my head?	Did I use a model?	Did I write down the numbers and solve it on paper?

A.

Write four 2-digit numbers.

B.

Write four 2-digit numbers.

Friday: Make Your Own Story

Write a word problem. Then, model it, write the equation and solve it.

Story

Model

Equation

Monday: True or False?

Students have to read and discuss which equations are true and which ones are false.

Tuesday: Vocabulary Tic Tac Toe

Students make up and play their own Tic Tac Toe game.

At the end of the game, go over the possible answers with the entire class. Have students discuss what they wrote as answers.

Wednesday: What Doesn't Belong?

Students make up their own What Doesn't Belong set and show and discuss it with a math partner.

Thursday: Number Talk

In this activity students get to choose their own numbers and make their own problems. Teacher asks students how they solved it. Answers will vary. Some students will do it in their head, others will do it on a model and some will write it down on paper.

Friday: Make Your Own Word Problem

Students have to write, model and solve their own problem.

Week 40 Activities

Monday: True or False?

Look at the problems and decide which ones are true and which ones are false.

	True or False
$5 + 10 = 45 - 30$	
$20 - 10 = 10 + 10$	
$50 = 150 - 50$	
$2 + 4 + 6 = 10 + 2$	
Make your own!	

Tuesday: Vocabulary Tic Tac Toe

Make your own.

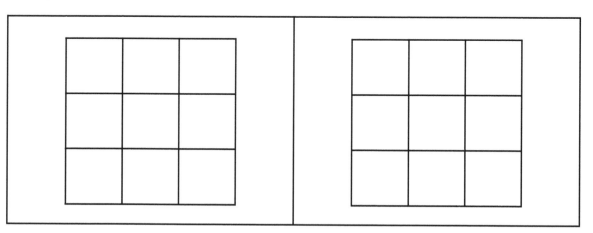

Wednesday: What Doesn't Belong?

Make your own. Discuss it with a math partner.

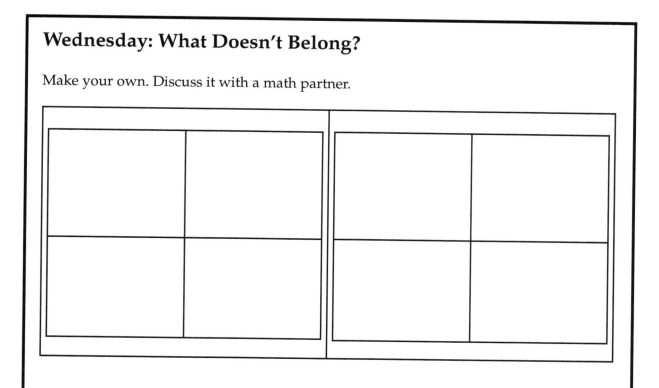

Thursday: Number Talk

Write numbers in each circle. Make problems. Solve them. Write the problem under the way you solved it.

Did I do it in my head?	Did I use a model?	Did I write down the numbers and solve it on paper?

A. Put 3 3-digit numbers.

B. Put 3 3-digit numbers.

Friday: Make Your Own Word Problem

Write a word problem. Model it. Solve it.

1. Story

2. Model

3. Equation

Answer Key

Week 1

Monday: What Doesn't Belong?

A. 8 + 4.

B. 7 – 5.

Tuesday: Vocabulary Match

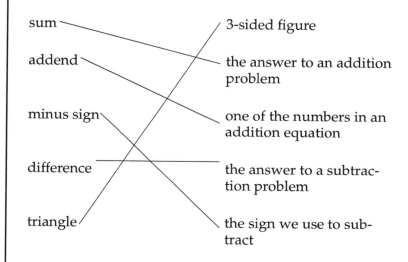

sum — the answer to an addition problem

addend — one of the numbers in an addition equation

minus sign — the sign we use to subtract

difference — the answer to a subtraction problem

triangle — 3-sided figure

Wednesday: Convince Me!

Answers vary.

Thursday: Number Talk

This is an opportunity for students to work on talking about addition of numbers. The focus should be on different strategies such as bridging ten, doubles plus two or doubles minus two.

Friday: What's the Question?

Answer vary.

For example: How many are there altogether?

Week 2

Monday: Magic Square

Answer should be 15 in every direction.

Tuesday: Vocabulary Tic Tac Toe

Answers vary. Students should have illustrations and definitions on the side.

Wednesday: Number Line It!

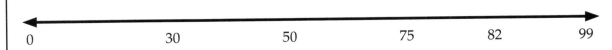

0	30	50	75	82	99

Thursday: Number Talk

Answers vary.

Friday: Sort the Problems

Answers vary. For example: John had 10 toy trucks. He gave away 5. How many does he have now?

Week 3

Monday: Always, Sometimes, Never

Sometimes, because when you add 0 the number stays the same.

Tuesday: Vocabulary It Is/It Isn't

Answers vary. For example: a hexagon is a polygon. A hexagon does not have curved sides.

Wednesday: Number of the Day

10

Number word. ten	Show 2 addition sentences that make ten. Answers vary. i.e. $8 + 2$
Show 2 subtraction sentences that make ten. Answers vary i.e. $10 - 0$	Add 3 numbers that make ten. Answers vary i.e. $2 + 3 + 5$

Thursday: Number Strings

Students work on solving the problem in different ways. The conversation should focus on bridging 10 when you add 7. This means that you would count up through ten and then on. For example, $7 + 5$ is $7 + 3 + 2$.

Friday: Model It

Students have to model the expression on a number line, Ten frame and by doing a math sketch.

Week 4

Monday: Find and Fix the Error

The answer is 2. Students should explain it and prove it with numbers, words and models.

Tuesday: Frayer Model

Students have to use the frayer model as a frame to discuss a rectangle. Answers vary.

Wednesday: Greater Than, Less Than, in Between

Students have to reason about numbers on their mental number line. Answers vary.

Thursday: Number Talk

Students discuss ways to do this subtraction problem. The emphasis is on talking about the strategies. Students should discuss how you could do partial differences, bridge back through ten (meaning you take 4 away to get to 10 and then 2 more) or think 6 + 6 is 12 and 2 more is 14 so the answer would be 8.

Friday: Picture That!

Students have to tell a story about the pictures. They can tell an addition or subtraction story. They should write a number sentence as well. Answers vary.

Week 5

Monday: 2 Arguments

Maria is correct.

Tuesday: Vocabulary Match

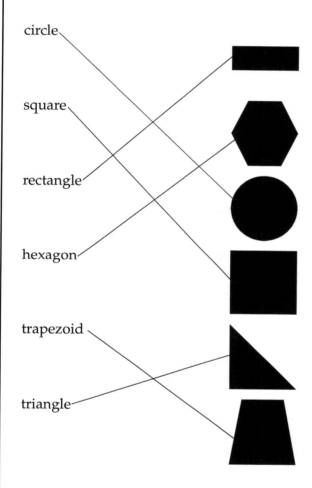

*Remember to discuss with students that a square is a special kind of rectangle as well.

Wednesday: Missing Numbers in a Hundred Grid

			47		
53	54	56	57	58	
	64		67		
73	74		77	78	
	84			88	89
	94				99

Thursday: Number Talk

Answers vary.

Students pick a number from each circle. They then discuss which strategy they used to solve the problem, either mental math, a model or computation with the numbers on paper.

Friday: Make Your Own Problem

Answers vary.

Students have to fill in the numbers and discuss the problem.

Week 6

Monday: Alike and Different

Answers vary.

Tuesday: Vocabulary 1-Minute Essay

Answers vary.

Wednesday: How Many More to

Start at 56. How many more to 70? 14

Start at 89. How many more to 100? 11

Start at 34. How many more to 50? 16

Thursday: Number Strings

Answers vary. For example, students should discus what happens when you bridge ten. They will talk about getting to the nearest ten and then adding on. 19 + 4 becomes 20 + 3 (take from 4 and give to 19).

Friday: Equation Match

B is the answer.

Week 7

Monday: 2 Arguments

Marvin is correct.

Tuesday: Vocabulary Brainstorm

Answers vary.

Wednesday: Guess My Number

A. 6.
B. 21.

Thursday: Number Talk

Answers vary. Students should be sure to talk about bridging the nearest 10 meaning 15 + 5 + 2. The answer is 22.

Friday: Equation Match

Problem B.

Week 8

Monday: True or False?

True. It has 6 straight sides, 6 angles and 6 vertices. It is a closed figure.

Tuesday: Vocabulary Tic Tac Toe

Answers vary.

Wednesday: Number Bond It

Answers vary.

Thursday: Number Talk

Answers vary. For example, teachers should make sure students talk about half facts, counting back if it is 1, 2 or 3, and bridging across 10. For example, 15 – 9 could be seen as 15 – 5 = 10. 10 – 4 = 6.

They could also do 15 – 10 = 5 and then add 1 back to get 6.

Friday: What's the Problem?

Jamal	7	
Mike	?	2

Week 9

Monday: Convince Me!

Answers vary.

Tuesday: It Is/It Isn't

Answers vary. For example: A pentagon is a polygon. It does not have curved sides.

Wednesday: Skip Counting

Skip counting by 2s. Answers vary.

Thursday: Number Strings

The discussion should focus on different strategies for subtracting 8 or 9 from a number such as making it a ten and then adding back 1 or 2. Or, adding 1 or 2 to each of the numbers to get a friendlier number.

Friday: What's the Question?

Answers vary.

Week 10

Monday: Reasoning Matrix

Jenny ate the chocolate pie.
Jamal ate the pecan pie.
Miguel ate the strawberry pie.
Kelly ate the lemon pie.

Tuesday: Vocabulary Tic Tac Toe

Answers vary.

Wednesday: Number of the Day

47

Word form Forty seven	10 more 57	10 less 37
Expanded form 40 + 7	____ + ____ = 47 Answers vary	____ − ____ = 47 Answers vary
Base ten sketch	How many more to 100? 53	Odd or even? odd

Thursday: Number Talk

Answers vary. Students could make the 17 a 20 and the 45 a 42. The answer is 62.

Students could do partial sums, adding a few numbers at a time. They could also do a "give and take strategy" where they made the 17 into a 20 and the 45 into 42 to get 62.

Friday: What's the Story?

Answers vary.

Week 11

Monday: Venn Diagram

There are boys and girls. The intersection is kids with glasses.

Students could sort in a variety of ways, but they are trying to find a way were there is an intersection.

Tuesday: What Doesn't Belong?

A. Clock.

B. Circle.

Wednesday: What's Missing?

25, **35**, **45**, 55, 65, 75, **80**

92, **94**, 96, **98**, **100**, 102, 104

50, **60**, **70**, **80**, 90, **100**, 110, 120, 130

Patterns vary.

Thursday: Number Talk

Answers vary. Students should talk about various addition strategies. For example, 35 + 9 can be seen as 35 + 10 − 1. 89 + 9 can be seen as 99 − 1.

Friday: What's the Question?

Answers vary. For example: How many more chocolate chip cookies were there than sugar cookies?

Week 12

Monday: Graph

Students should fill in the graph correctly. Questions vary.

Tuesday: Frayer Model

Answers vary.

Wednesday: Compose it

Answers vary.

Thursday: Number Talk

Answers vary. Discussion should center around taking the ones from a teen number.

Friday: Make Your Own Problem

Students have to make up their own problem.

Week 13

Monday: What Doesn't Belong?

A. Difference.

B. $3 + 7 + 5$.

Tuesday: Frayer Model

Answers vary.

Wednesday: Legs and Feet

1. 8.
2. 1 cricket and 2 chickens.
3. 2 crickets and 1 chicken or 4 chickens and 1 cricket.

Thursday: Number Talk

Strategies vary. The answer is 7.

Students should talk about different ways to think about this problem. They could think of doubles and see this as a half fact. They could count back 4 and then 3 more.

Friday: Model That!

Students should model the problem. The answer is 7.

Week 14

Monday: Always, Sometimes, Never

Sometimes. Some teachers are 22 and 23. 7 + 15 is 22. So some teachers are only 15 or 16 years older than 2nd graders.

Tuesday: Vocabulary Bingo

Answers vary.

Wednesday: Guess My Number

A. 110.

B. 31.

Thursday: Number Talk

Answers vary. For example: 7 + 6 or 4 + 5.

It is important for students to understand the concept of double plus 1, so the teacher might illustrate this with manipulatives. Students should understand that any 2 numbers that sit side by side on the number line make a double plus 1 fact. For example, 3 + 4 is really 3 + 3 + 1 more.

Friday: Math Story

Stories vary.

For example: The bakery had 18 lollipops. They sold 14. How many do they have left?

Models vary.

Equation: 18 − 14 = 4.

Week 15

Monday: How Many More to

How many more to 20?

5 add 15
8 add 12
9 add 11
12 add 8
17 add 3

Tuesday: Vocabulary Fill-in

A. quadrilateral.
B. hexagon.
C. polygon.
D. circle.

Wednesday: What Doesn't Belong?

A. 10 − 4 isn't a half fact.
B. 9 + 1 isn't a doubles plus 1 fact.

Thursday: Number Strings

Answers vary.

Students should understand how to do this in their head because it is a first grade standard. However, the teacher might need to model this with base ten blocks, sketches or the hundred grid.

Friday: Model in the Part-Part Whole Mat

Whole 18	
Part	Part
9	9

Week 16

Monday: Reasoning Matrices

Sue likes butterflies.
Carl likes crickets.
Lucy likes frogs.

Tuesday: Vocabulary Bingo

Answers vary.

Wednesday: Missing Numbers

Fill in the missing numbers from the hundreds chart.

		95	96	97	
103	104	105		107	
	114			117	118

Thursday: Number Talk

Answers vary. Students should share strategies. For example, students should discuss breaking apart numbers and adding the tens and then the ones, making tens and counting up.

So 29 + 14 would become 30 + 13 because we took 1 from 14 to make 29 into a 30 so the problem would be easier.

Students should share strategies. For example, students should discuss breaking apart numbers and adding the tens and then the ones, making tens and counting up.

So 29 + 14 would become 30 + 13 because we took 1 from 14 to make 29 into a 30 so the problem would be easier.

Friday: Model That!

There are 10 lady bugs. Models vary.

Week 17

Monday: 2 Arguments

Kelly is correct because 13 + 7 equals 20.

Tuesday: Vocabulary Bingo

Answers vary.

Wednesday: Missing Numbers in a Two Hundred Grid

141		143	144	145			148		
151	152	153		**155**			158	159	
	162			165	166	167	168		170

Thursday: Number Talk

Answers vary. For example: 7 + 8 or 30 − 15.

Friday: 3 Questions

Answers vary. For example How many pieces of fruit are there altogether?

How many more bananas would we need to have the same amount as we do of apples?

Week 18

Monday: True or False?

A. False.

B. True.

C. Answers vary.

Tuesday: What Doesn't Belong?

A. 20 + 20 + 40. We could also say that 100 − 30 doesn't belong because it is a subtraction problem. B. 3 + 2 is not a doubles plus 2 fact.

Wednesday: Guess My Number

A. Answers vary.

B. Answers vary.

For example:

It is more than 5.

It is less than 10.

It is an odd number.

Thursday: Number Strings

The discussion should focus on what happens when you add 10 to a number.

Friday: Model That!

They saw 6 fish and 14 animals altogether.

Week 19

Monday: Missing Numbers

Answers vary.

$5 + 2 = 5 + 2$

$4 + 2 = 5 + 1$

Tuesday: Vocabulary Bingo

Answers vary.

Wednesday: Number Bond It!

Answers vary.

Thursday: Number Talk

Answers vary. Students should discuss subtraction strategies. For example, $21 - 18$ could be $21 - 20$ which is 1 and then add 2 back which makes 3. Or count up from 18 to 21. $62 - 13$ could be $62 - 10$ which is 52 and then take away 3 more to get 49.

Friday: What's the Story?

Answers vary.

For example:

There were 2 boxes of oranges. They each had 15 oranges. How many oranges were there altogether?

Models vary.

$15 + 15 = 30$

Week 20

Monday: True or False?

	True or False?
$8 + 10 = 4 + 5 + 5 + 4$	true
$12 - 6 = 20 - 14$	true
$20 = 15 - 5$	false
$5 - 5 = 10 - 5$	false
Make your own!	answers vary

Tuesday: Vocabulary Tic Tac Toe

Answers vary.

Wednesday: What Doesn't Belong?

A. Rectangular prism.

B. $80 - 10$

We could also say $4 + 6$ doesn't belong because it is the only addition example.

Thursday: Number Strings

Answers vary. Students should be talking about bridging through 10 when you have 7, 8 or 9. This means that they would take away enough to get back to ten and then take away the rest. For example, $15 - 7$ can be done as $15 - 5$ gets you to 10 and then $- 2$ more gets you to 8. Or $17 - 8$ could be $17 - 7$ gets you to 10 and then take away 1 more which gets you to 9. Or kids can use a count up strategy. For example, 8 plus 2 is 10 and then 7 more to 17 and then add the 2 jumps of 2 and 7 which is 9.

Friday: Problem Solving

There are 10 fish and 15 animals altogether.

Week 21

Monday: What Doesn't Belong?

A. 100 – 40

You could also so 60 – 30 because it is a half fact.

B. 20 + 60. You could also say 35 + 35 because it is the only doubles fact.

Tuesday: Vocabulary Tic Tac Toe

Answers vary.

Wednesday: Convince Me!

Answers vary.

Thursday: Number Strings

Answers vary. So 81 – 19 would become 82 – 20, which is a much easier problem to solve.

Students should be working on using various subtraction strategies, such as compensation, same difference, partial sums and counting up. For example, for same difference, you can add 1 to each number. 81 – 19 would become 82 –20, which is a much easier problem.

Friday: Model It

Katy has 7 stickers.

Week 22

Monday: Magic Squares

A.

8	3	4
1	5	9
6	7	2

B.

6	1	8
7	5	3
2	9	4

Tuesday: Vocabulary Tic Tac Toe

Answers vary.

Wednesday: Number Line It!

⟵————————————————————————⟶

0   19   42   51   67   83   99 100

Thursday: Number Talk

Answers vary.

Friday: Word Problem Sort

1. Addition 20.
2. Subtraction 35.
3. Addition 89.
4. Addition 10.

Week 23

Monday: Always, Sometimes, Never

Sometimes. Students should have to reason this out and give examples with explanations. For example, 24 + 25 is 49 which is not even.

Tuesday: Vocabulary Bingo

Answers vary.

Wednesday: Number of the Day

78

Number in word form. Seventy-eight	Show 1 addition sentence that makes 78. Answers vary i.e. 77 +1
Show 1 subtraction sentence that makes 78. Answers vary, i.e. 79 – 1	Add 3 numbers that make 78. Answers vary, i.e. 20 + 30 + 28

Thursday: Number Strings

Answers vary.

Discussion should include talking about getting to a ten to make friendly numbers. For example, 17 + 6 can become 20 + 3.

Friday: Model That!

The answer is 61.

Week 24

Monday: Magic Square

8	1	6
3	5	7
4	9	2

Tuesday: It Is/It Isn't

Answers vary. For example it is a 2-digit number. It is not even.

Wednesday: Greater Than, Less Than, in Between

Answers vary.

Thursday: Number Talk

35. Discussion should include talking about making the problem friendly by using a 10. For example, 55 – 20 (made by adding 1 to each number) equals 35.

Friday: Picture That!

Answers vary.

Week 25

Monday: 2 Arguments

Maya is correct because 12 + 38 is 50.

Tuesday: Vocabulary Draw

Answers vary.

Wednesday: Money Problems

Answers vary. For example, students could draw a quarter or 2 dimes and a nickel.

Thursday: Number Talk

Answers vary.

Friday: Make Your Own Problem

Answers vary.

Week 26

Monday: It Is/It Isn't

Answers vary. For example: A rectangle is a polygon. It does not have open sides.

Tuesday: Vocabulary Quick Write

Students should write about how all polygons have straight, closed sides, angles and vertices.

Wednesday: Find and Fix the Error

The mistake is that John added instead of subtracting.

Thursday: Number Strings

Students are looking at patterns in expressions.
The focus in this conversation is bridging 10 when there is a 7, 8 or 9.

Friday: Equation Match

The answer is B.

Week 27

Monday: 3 Truths and a Fib

50 is greater than 100 is the fib.

Tuesday: Vocabulary Brainstorm

Answers vary.

Wednesday: Complete the Pattern

1. 110, 210, **310, 410, 510**, 610, **710**
2. 55, **65**, 75, **85**, 95, **105**, 115, **125, 135**
3. Answers vary.

Thursday: Number Talk

Students discuss subtracting this expression by counting up or subtracting back or finding the same difference on the number line to make the problem easier by adding 2 to each number.

Friday: What's the Story?

The answer is B.

Week 28

Monday: True or False?

True.

Tuesday: Vocabulary Tic Tac Toe

Answers vary.

Wednesday: Reasoning Missing numbers

A. 23 + 55.

B. 52 + 48.

Thursday: Number Talk

Answers vary.

Friday: Model That!

Hong | 5 | 5 | 5 | 5 | 5 |

?

Joe | 5 |

Hong had 25. Joe had 5. Together they had 30.

Week 29

Monday: Convince Me!

Answers vary.

Tuesday: Vocabulary Talk

Answers vary.

Wednesday: Skip Counting

Answers vary.

Thursday: Number Strings

Students work on subtracting 10 and 100 from numbers.

Friday: What's the Story?

Answers vary. The answer is that there are 12 pineapples.

Week 30

Monday: Magic Square

6	1	8
7	5	3
2	9	4

Tuesday: Vocabulary Tic Tac Toe

Answers vary.

Wednesday: Number of the Day.

507

Word Form Five hundred and seven	10 more 517	10 less 497
Expanded form $500 + 7$	_____ + _____ = 507 Answers vary.	_____ − _____ = 507 Answers vary
Base ten sketch □ □ □ □ □	How many more to 1,000 493	Odd or even? odd
100 more 607	100 less 407	$507 -$ _____ $=$ _____ Answers vary

Thursday: Number Talk

$457 + 335 = 792.$ $481 + 519 = 1,000$

Friday: What's the Story?

Answers vary. For example: There were 60 apples and 40 oranges. How many pieces of fruit were there altogether?

Week 31

Monday: Venn Diagram

Students populate the Venn diagram. Answers vary.

Tuesday: Vocabulary Bingo

Answers vary.

Wednesday: Why Is It Not?

A. It is not 18 because 18 + 6 does not make 12.

B. It is not 8 because 8 − 2 does not equal 10.

Thursday: Number Talk

A. 72 + 61 = 133.

B. 498 + 502 = 1000.

Friday: What's the Question?

Answers vary. For example: How many cookies were there altogether?

Another question could be: How many fewer chocolate cookies were there than lemon ones?

Week 32

Monday: Magic Square

2	7	6
9	5	1
4	3	8

Tuesday: Vocabulary Brainstorm

Answers vary.

Wednesday: 3 Truths and a Fib

900 + 10 is 1,000 is a fib.

Thursday: Number Talk

Students discuss subtracting include using various strategies, such as partial differences, compensation (adding a number to each number to get an easier problem), and counting up.

The answer is 582.

Friday: Word Problem Sort

B is the compare problem. Her sister has 15 rings.

Week 33

Monday: What Doesn't Belong?

A. 4:30 doesn't belong.

B. 8:00 doesn't belong.

Tuesday: Frayer Model

Answers vary.

Wednesday: Number of the Day

443

Word form Four hundred forty three	10 more 453	10 less 433
expanded form 400 + 40 + 3	_____ + _____ = 443 Answers vary	_____ − _____ = 443 Answers vary
Base ten sketch 	How many more to 1,000 557	Odd or even? odd
100 more 543	100 less 343	443 − _____ = _____ Answers vary.

Thursday: Number Talk

Students should talk about subtraction strategies such as counting up, partial differences and compensation (making friendly numbers).

Friday: What's the Question?

Answers vary. For example: How many fewer red marbles are there than green ones.

How many marbles are there all together?

Week 34

Monday: Convince Me!

Explanations vary. Students should be able to explain why and give examples. For example, if you add 2 and 3 you will get 5. 2 and 2 would give you 4 but you have 1 extra with 2 and 3 so you will get an odd number.

Tuesday: Frayer Model

Answers vary.

Wednesday: Guess My Number

A. 27.
B. 82.

Thursday: Number Talk

Students discuss addition strategies such as break apart and friendly numbers. In this case students could add $100 + 200$ and then $80 + 40$ and then $8 + 9$. Also, students could make 188 into 200 and then just add 237 to that number.

Friday: Picture That!

Answers vary.

Week 35

Monday: Tic Tac Toe

Answers vary.

Tuesday: Vocabulary Fill-in

a. sum.
b. array.
c. difference.
d. even.

Wednesday: Missing Numbers

A. 586 + 204 = 790.

B. 182 + 719 = 901.

Thursday: Number Talk

Students are reasoning about the difference between numbers. Listen to their thinking and their strategies for coming up with the differences.

Friday: What's the Question?

Answers vary. For example: How many fewer footballs are there than soccer balls?

Week 36

Monday: What Doesn't Belong?

A. 2 + 38 makes 40 and the others make 38.

40 – 2 is the only subtraction problem and 19 + 19 is the only doubles.

B. 1,000 – 250.

Tuesday: Vocabulary 1-Minute Essay

Answers vary.

Wednesday: Fraction of the Day

$$\frac{1}{4}$$

Word form	Rectangle model
one-fourth	
Circle model	Non-example circle

Thursday: Number Talk

A. Answers vary. For example, 199 – 98 is about a difference of 100.

B. Answers vary. For example 500 – 245 has a difference of about 250.

Friday: Make up Your Own Story

Answers vary. For example: Jamil had 14 marbles and he got 3 more. How many does he have now?

14 + 3 = 17

Week 37

Monday: Number Bond It!

Answers vary

Tuesday: Vocabulary 1-Minute Essay

Answers vary.

Wednesday: Fraction of the Day

$$\frac{1}{2}$$

word form half	rectangle model
circle model 	non-example Answers vary. For example $\frac{1}{4}$.

Thursday: Number Talk

Answers vary.

Friday: Make Your Own Problem

Answers vary. For example: Mike had 15 marbles. Greg had 3 more than he did. How many did Greg have?

Week 38

Monday: Graphs

Students must complete the graph correctly. Questions and answers vary. For example: How many more dogs are there than cats? How many people voted altogether?

Tuesday: Vocabulary Tic Tac Toe

Answers vary.

Wednesday: Missing Numbers

Answers vary.

Thursday: Number Talk

Answers vary.

Friday: Make up Your Own Story

2 fish came.
There are 12 animals altogether.

Week 39

Monday: Graphs

Students have to complete the graph correctly. Questions and answers vary. For example: How many people voted altogether? How many fewer people liked cats than dogs.

Tuesday: Vocabulary Math Tic Tac Toe

Answers vary.

Wednesday: Number Bond It!

Answers vary.

Thursday: Number Talk

Answers vary.

Friday: Make Your Own Story
Answers vary.

Week 40

Monday: True or False?

	True or False
$5 + 10 = 45 - 30$	true
$20 - 10 = 10 + 10$	false
$50 = 150 - 50$	false
$2 + 4 + 6 = 10 + 2$	true
Make your own!	answers vary

Tuesday: Vocabulary Tic Tac Toe

 Answer vary.

Wednesday: What Doesn't Belong?

Answers vary.

Thursday: Number Talk

Answers vary.

Friday: Make Your Own Story

Answers vary.